The God Who Heals

One Woman's Journey of Healing After Facing
Some of Life's Most Difficult Challenges

Julie Mae Anderson

Want to go even deeper and experience healing as you embark on my journey with me?

As my thank you for reading, I'd like to gift you *The God Who Heals Study Guide*, a 16-week companion bible study guide that was created to go along with this book.

This study guide is perfect to help you reflect on your own life and understand how God wants to speak to you. It provides questions related to each chapter to ponder where you are in your circumstances and how God will guide you. It can help you heal from past issues and traumas as you give them over to God in complete surrender and learn to forgive the ones that may have hurt you.

You will also find a great resource that can be used for asking additional Biblical questions that may not have been addressed in your situation. Look for this resource in Chapters 6 and 7 of the study guide.

Get *The God Who Heals Study Guide* at bwicministries.com/studyguide.

The God Who Heals
Copyright © 2024 Julie Anderson in Association with Butterfly Books Publishing

Cover Design by I Love My Cover Designs
Interior Design and Typesetting by Butterfly Books Publishing
Edited and Proofread by Butterfly Books Publishing

ISBN (paperback): 979-8-9905662-5-5
ISBN (hardcover): 979-8-9905662-6-2

Printed in the United States of America.

Scripture quotations noted NIV are from the LIFE APPLICATION BIBLE: NEW INTERNATIONAL VERSION® Copyright © 1988, 1989, 1990, 1991 by Tyndale House Publishers, Inc. Wheaton, IL 60189. All rights reserved.

This is a true story. The events and conversations in this book have been set down to the best of the author's ability, although some names and details have been changed to protect the privacy of individuals.

Reviews From Readers:

Julie has gone through so many difficulties this far in her life where her faith has kept her strong. Her perseverance is so inspiring and has been a huge inspiration to me. I am amazed with her positivity and know that it comes from her faith in our Lord. I feel that she teaches this so well with how she goes through not only her most difficult times but also through her everyday life. My life has improved greatly after reading her story as I use her experiences and strength through faith as an example of how to handle my life's trials. I highly recommend this book as it is an amazing story of difficult times and the strength to overcome.

- L. O., Iowa

The author, Julie Anderson, shared her life of persistence and fortitude of what she had been given of her assignment. She had setbacks but that did not stop her. She kept moving forward one step at a time as she bear the pain from the adversity. As you read her story you will be drawn to the excitement of what is on the next page, next chapter, as she returns to her first love.

- M. V., Illinois

I have the privilege of knowing both Julie and the biological mother of her son. After hearing the amazing intricacies of their story, I knew God's hand was all over it. When God says in Romans 8:28, "and we know that all things work together for good to them that love God, to them who are called according to His purpose," this was it! For God to move in all circumstances and make an unwanted pregnancy give glory to Him, wow! He also says in Psalms 139:13-14, "for you created my inmost being, You knit me together in my mother's womb." He does! There is no doubt that God's sovereign hand was in this story. I highly recommend you read and see how God can take impossible situations and turn them around for His glory and yours. Oh, how He loves us!

- L.J. T., Texas

I just finished reading *The God Who Heals* by Julie Anderson and her life story is written from her heart about her life, struggles, failures, successes, dreams, and hope for her future. She is very honest and open. She shares about her hopes and dreams, her future endeavors in trainings, and new ministries helping others grow in Christ. I look forward to reading her new releases as her vision for changing people's lives spiritually, emotionally, and physically, including having the resources for their daily lives, takes shape.

- G. G., Wisconsin

I enjoyed her story, *The God Who Heals*! In the first chapter, titled, *In the Beginning*, you are personally introduced to her grandparents and parents. And throughout her story, you meet family and friends and others who each have their own impact on her story. I reflected naturally on my own attitudes, beliefs, feelings, judgments, and thoughts. You will too. Please take care of yourself and May God Bless You. Amen.

- C. J., Wisconsin

Contents

FOREWORD

I got connected to Julie through a mutual friend shortly before the release of her book, but all I can say is that it felt like a perfect example of how God brings and works things together.

Ever since the fall of man, humanity has been in a cycle of longing for the way things were originally made to be – created by God in the garden of Eden – and yet unable to break free from the curse of sin that has affected not just us, but all of creation.

We can see the effects of it all around us every day. The sick, the dying, those who are suffering, loss, pain, tragedy, difficulty, opposition, trauma, brutality, even the most unspeakable things. But beyond the pain we humans experience and cause each other, we see it in nature too. Animals fighting and killing each other, earthquakes and other natural disasters that ravage the land and people's lives.

So, what do we do? Is there a solution? Are we doomed to repeating these cycles repeatedly, hoping that maybe somehow, we humans will finally attain what we long for through our technological advances or by somehow making peace with each other?

It is said that those who do not learn from the past are doomed to repeat it. History can tell that despite humanity's best efforts, repeat the cycle we do.

Yet, there is a solution, a light, a way to overcome. And He made the way by doing everything oppositely from what the world says to do.

Others would say that if you were hurt, then you would hurt back. Get revenge. Fight for what you want. Get everything you can.

Jesus says, "Come to me all who are weary and heavy laden, and I will give you rest." He promises that when you cast your cares on Him that He cares for you. He even promises that vengeance belongs to Him. True, righteous, holy. Jesus says the Heavenly Father will give you everything you need freely when you surrender to Him and delight yourself in Him. Because He died and conquered death and sin for you to be reconciled to Him!

It is a little backwards, isn't it? Surrender to win?

But yes, when we hand over ourselves and say, "Your will be done," that's actually where the greatest, miraculous wonders start to take place. Healing, transformation, growth, real change, and believe it or not, the type of outcomes we humans long for. Eternal life. Joy, hope, peace, love. These are intangible things in a way, but they are the very things that your soul actually longs for, was made for.

What I love about Julie's story is how she faced so many things in her life and yet how passionate she is about sharing love, hope, faith, and healing with as many people as she can. Her story is one that inspires an eagerness to lean into the Lord, seek Him with all your heart, learn to hear His voice again, and embrace His grace and forgiveness deeper every day.

It's so easy to go through difficult, even impossible things and come out the other side broken, angry, selfish, and completely rejecting of God.

But in *The God Who Heals*, Julie reminds every person that the pain and suffering we experience is not the end. It's not for nothing. And God is with you in every moment. He is there for you. He will not fail you. And He can heal your every part.

Don't believe me?

Well, read it for yourself.

But don't just read it. Dive in. Ponder. Reflect. Do the study guide.

Your life will never be the same in all the best ways.

Katelyn Silva
Founder & CEO, We Write Books
5x Bestselling Author
Butterfly Books Publishing

PROLOGUE

As I quietly sat in my softly lit room on my bed contemplating about preparing a draft for this book, I scrolled through some photos, predicting which picture I could use for the cover. Instantly captivated by the photo with steps leading up the mountainside, I knew it was the perfect one. When I took a closer look, it seemed as if the stairs were heading into the unknown. This is a place where I seemed to have lived on my healing journey.

It suddenly reminded me of all the unknowns in my life. The steps were some of the hurts and struggles I endured on my healing journey with the Lord Jesus Christ. I thought to myself, '*Hmm! This would be the perfect cover for the book, and will the steps I faced and the healing I received help someone else? I should share my story!*'

The process of my healing journey was not always easy because of the unknown attached to the fear that lay before me. "Do I stay, or do I go?" would play over and over in my mind when I had to decide. It took faith in God to take that next step up the mountainside to slowly reach my goal of true and lasting peace.

Each step in my journey was hard to climb, especially when I wanted to give up. I remember the time when I finally said to myself, "No, I will not do that. I'm done! I have had enough heartache. I will do it myself." But without looking to God for the answers, I left Him out of the choice I made which resulted in a BIG, MASSIVE, HUGE mistake. I did it my way! I took matters into my own hands because of my impatience to wait. When I look back, I think, '*Why did I have to move ahead of God? If I had taken my time and eagerly waited on Him, I might not have missed what could have been.*' But God is faithful to use our experiences in a way that can still bring glory to Him and can help others who may be going through the same things.

The healing process can be difficult. Reflecting on the pain from the past, I thought, *'How can I move forward if I am still in an emotional wreck about the BIG, MASSIVE, HUGE mistake I made? I needed to trust God to be in complete control of all the situations I have been through.'* God has a better plan for each of us if we learn to let go and let God.

Over time, different emotions filled my heart from sadness, depression, loss, discouragement to joy, happiness, fulfillment. and finally, the peace God brings that surpasses all understanding. Here is my story!

Chapter One

IN THE BEGINNING

It all began with the Creator of the World. God created each of us to love and trust Him wholeheartedly. He is the God who knows everything about every person and yet still loves them. He can use anyone and anything to reach a hurtful world. He is the Great Physician and Healer of *all* wounds.

This is the story of a little girl's life that was radically changed on a journey with God from the beginning but did not know it until later in life. He healed her through traumatic events that took place over the years. He never wasted anything she went through as He can bring beauty from ashes. All the names were changed in this story to protect the innocent.

The story of this girl's life begins with two teenagers who lived in Wisconsin: Harry and Sally. Even though they were having intimate relations, they were not thinking *it* could ever happen to them. Then the unexpected happened! She got pregnant.

Sally's mind raced with thoughts, *'(OMG) Oh My God! What am I going to do now? Do I keep it, abort it, or give it away? How am I going to tell my parents?'*

After weeks of stressing over her dilemma, Sally finally got up the nerve to tell her parents. And in the 1940s, pregnancy, if not married, was unacceptable and very shameful to the family's reputation. And she was not married. Harry wanted her to abort the baby, but her parents made her surrender the child for adoption by moving her to another city in Wisconsin to hide the shame. Alone and abandoned, Sally struggled through the pregnancy.

Two years later, Sally's mother strongly suggested Sally marry Harry. Her mother felt he was a good catch and that she should never let him go. Sally agreed to do it but was not happy about the arrangement. During the marriage, she gave birth to four more children: two girls and a set of twins – a boy and a girl. Her life focuses became her children's wellbeing and running a household that could get chaotic sometimes with four very active little ones.

Already feeling busy trying to manage her little ones and home, she found out she was expecting another child. With the marriage already struggling from other tensions, she did not want to add another child into the mix. It made Sally feel completely overwhelmed and overworked.

She decided it would be best if she self-aborted the baby. Afterward, thinking that the abortion was successful, she continued with her life taking care of the family. But God, however, had a different plan.

One summer morning several months later, the sun was shining, and the soft wind was blowing, and it happened. The contractions of childbirth were beginning to take place. The ambulance was called, and Sally was rushed to the hospital. Being that this was not her first child, the urgency to get to the emergency room was crucial. She could have her baby any minute.

As she waited for the doctor to arrive to assess the condition, she practiced the breathing technique taught by the Lamaze Classes she had attended. The contractions kept coming closer and closer – within seconds! It was time to push and push she did. The delivery of this newly developed child in her womb began. It was August, and there was the sound of the newborn baby's cry. A baby girl named Julie Mae. The siblings all waited patiently at the front door for this bundle of joy to enter the home, the newest family member, me.

From that moment on, things got more difficult in the homestead. There was another mouth to feed and more clothes to buy. Plus, the added burden of running a household with laundry, cooking, cleaning, and getting kids ready for school. It was getting to be too much for Sally to handle and she took it out on the kids. So, there was some physical abuse that started to take place.

My mom, Sally, was incredibly stressed out. Things were not pleasant, and she was sad from the relationship she had with my dad. He worked long hours and sometimes would not come home until extremely late in the evening to be with the family. When he got home, there would be yelling and fighting about him being out and she often accused him of being with other women while she was home taking care of the five kids. My sisters and my brother coped the best they could while I was too young to understand what was truly taking place.

One day Sally had enough. My oldest sister caught her with another man on the couch. *She* was the one cheating, not dad. My oldest sister, age seven at the time, told dad what she saw during the day. Well, more fighting and yelling took place and dad kicked Sally out of the house. She had no choice but to leave the family and venture out on her own with me in tow. She loved me and feared I would be at risk of neglect if she left me behind. She was not able to take the rest of my siblings with her because of her own lack of financial means and a place to live.

Sally and I moved in with her parents, and eventually she got a job working in a factory. She asked her mother to watch me while she went to work. During that time, dad kept trying to get me back but was not having any success. Until one day when Sally's mother called dad and said, "Come and get your daughter because I have a doctor's appointment and can't take her with me."

Dad thought, *'Great, this would be a perfect opportunity to take my two-year-old daughter home with me to live with the rest of the siblings.'* So, he agreed to come and get me.

When Sally found out, she was devastated! However, because she was not emotionally strong enough to fight for me, she moved to California by herself to get as far away from it all as possible. She decided she was going to start her life over in a new place and leave everything behind and forget about the past and her children.

Our grandma, dad's mom, while she was in her late 50s, moved from Wisconsin to Illinois to help him raise his five children. We were never allowed to talk to Sally again because dad was hurt over what she had done. In his eyes, she was considered dead.

I was now at the age of five; it was finally time for me to start attending school. I was so excited. I would sit home with grandma thinking about what it would be like to go to school. One of the fun things I looked forward to doing was to ride the bus to school. My siblings shared how a person could feel every bump in the road when sitting in the back of the bus and could bounce high in the air when the wheels hit it. I was ready for this ride and my first day at school. I could hardly wait!

The Christian school we attended went from kindergarten until eighth grade. Connected to the school was the church we attended every weekend where we learned about who God was. I even participated in the choir for the wrong reasons. I had a crush on one of the guys in my sister's class; he was also part of the choir. But he never was interested in me because of the height difference. I was taller than him and it must have intimidated him.

On special occasions, I noticed there were room moms that came into the classroom to help with parties, birthdays, and holiday celebrations. It broke my heart deeply because I longed for a mother to love me and be in the classroom like the other moms. But there was none.

As time went on, I wondered, '*Will I ever experience life with a mother figure again?*'

Three years passed before dad found the woman he wanted to marry. Being eight years old at the time, I was excited to finally have a mom to love me.

The new marriage brought with it four more children, all girls. The once family of six instantly became a family of eleven, with eight girls and one boy. The age spans between the nine of us siblings were only five years. At one point, there were nine teenagers in the home with only one bathroom. Imagine being the only boy getting ready in the morning with eight girls fighting over the bathroom mirror and shower. Somehow, we made it work and arrived at school on time.

Upon graduating elementary school, the family became church CEOs (Christmas and Easter Only) attenders. I knew a little about God from the classes that were taught in school, but never had a personal relationship with Him. After finishing at the public High School, we stopped attending church as a family. Never talked about it again.

I was no longer that cute little girl, with curls tight to my head, but a tall, slender, young woman with high hopes for my future. After graduating from high school, I attended a travel school in Florida to pursue a career as a cruise director. I got the idea from watching the television show "The Love Boat." To me being a cruise director looked like a wonderful opportunity to meet people and supply fun activities for everyone to enjoy. But I later found out I got seasick. That dream came to a quick end, and I had to find other avenues to use my travel degree.

When I returned home with my degree in hand, my dad encouraged me to keep seeking a job in this newfound field. I called different airline companies. The closest airline, Mississippi Valley Airlines, was hiring a reservation specialist. It was only a couple of hours away from where I lived, which would allow me the ability to go home for the holidays and special occasions.

Dad would ask every time he came home from work, "Did you call that airline back yet?"

I would reply, "No, dad, but I will."

I began calling the airline daily, and after weeks of calls, persistence paid off. The airline company finally hired me as their new reservation specialist. The job was in the Quad Cities, and I rented a place with a coworker not too far from the job. No longer was I living at home. I was on my own at the age of eighteen in a strange town with no friends. It was a little scary being on my own at a young age, but also freeing as well, no longer bound by family rules, and I could do what I wanted without being told, "You can't do that."

Things in my life were going smoothly. I was enjoying the job where I was working. I slowly made friends in the area.

And one day while working out, I met the man of my dreams. Jon. He was tall, dark, and handsome, my knight in shining armor. He was the janitor that took care of the YMCA. He was ten years my senior, but I did not mind.

I remember the day he invited me to a party his roommate was having. I agreed to go, but the day I went, I was having a hard time finding the place. Eventually, somehow, I was able to find the house. It was as if I was led there or maybe it was fate? While at the party, I had these feelings inside me that I had never felt before toward a man. It was as if I had cheerful butterflies stirring in my stomach. After the party, he gave me my first kiss and I saw fireworks. It was meant to be. We spent lots of time together. It was fun to be around him, and we enjoyed doing things together. We were in love and that was all that mattered. We spent our free time working out, running short distances, hiking, and other fun activities.

I continued working for the airline for one more year until the company merged with Air Wisconsin Airline. Because of the merger, if I wanted to stay with the company, I would have to move to Wisconsin, a strange place, leaving the familiar, and the man of my dreams, to go to the unknown. I would also have to leave my family since they were not that far away. Moving to colder weather, longer distance away from everyone. It was a big decision.

"Do I stay, or do I go?" played in my mind repeatedly, "What do I do?" *'I need the job, but do I move to Wisconsin?'* It would cause a long-distance relationship with my family and possibly mean saying good-bye to my knight in shining armor forever. It was a sad day choosing what to do. I made the decision to move and hoped for the best, trusting that I was doing the right thing. I transferred with the merger to Wisconsin.

The new airline, Air Wisconsin, had a contest that whoever booked the most connecting flights with Delta Airlines would receive a free ticket on Delta. I, being extremely competitive, worked hard to earn that free ticket.

I had recently found out some information about my birthmother. She had moved to Texas and was living with her new husband, Joey. Since I had not seen her for 18 years, I decided it would be nice to visit her for the first time in Texas and I would use the free winning ticket to go see her.

As I waited to hear if I had won the contest, the excitement and anticipation increased every day. The day came for them to announce the winner. My heart raced one hundred miles a minute, faster than I ever thought possible!

I thought, *'Will I hear them call my name?'*

They picked me! I was so excited that I jumped up and down shouting loudly, "I get to go see her. I get to go see my mom for the first time in 18 years!" The emotions were so strong that it brought tears to my eyes.

I was the winner of the free ticket. Excitedly, I, at once, booked a flight to Texas for a month away. The weeks of anticipation of the visit turned into days and the days into minutes; then finally the time came to see my mother. More excitement filled my heart.

I thought, *'What is this going to be like? Will I know who my mother is? Will we have a good connection? Will my mother know me? Will I be able to find her in the airport?'*

I recognized her right away because she looked like me and welcomed me with a big hug. An embrace needed from her for years. It caused an instant connection and a joyful feeling inside that I had my mother back in my life. This started the beginning of the healing journey of my heart.

During the week-long remarkable vacation, I found out that my mother got pregnant as a teenager and placed her daughter, Sarah, up for adoption.

When I returned home from the trip, I was full of curiosity about knowing who Sarah was. Surprisingly, Sarah contacted our family shortly after that. She lived in Wisconsin. Since I also now lived in Wisconsin, I realized she could not be too far from me.

Another day of expectation came.

I thought, '*Will we look alike? Will she be happy to meet me, too?*'

My newfound sibling looked almost exactly like me. You would know we were sisters. We were the only two with the same color hair in the family, because God created us that way. It also made me feel like I was no longer the odd ball in the family with a different color hair. I always wondered if I was the mailman's daughter. Just kidding!

"You formed my innermost being, shaping my delicate inside and my intricate outside, and wove them all together in my mother's womb. I, thank You, God for making me so mysteriously complex! Everything You do is marvelously breathtaking. It simply amazes me to think about it! How thoroughly You know me, Lord."
Psalm 139:13-14, TPT

Chapter Two

THE UNEXPECTED

Remember that tall dark and handsome man of my dreams, Jon? He came to visit me during the fall season after I had moved to Wisconsin. We had a fantastic time together walking along the marina, hiking in the woods, and just hanging out taking memorable pictures.

After leaving me, he thought to himself, *'This is the lady I want to spend the rest of my life with.'*

Two months later, I visited him, and he asked me to marry him.

With an excited response, the answer was, "Yes, I would love to be your wife!"

The day of our wedding came with much anticipation. The day every young lady looks forward to experiencing. It was a happy joyous day. Everything went perfectly from the dress to the flowers to the pictures with my family. All of it!

As I look back now, as I write my story, I didn't know at the time that it would be the last picture of our whole family ever being together as a group again. It will be a cherished photo to keep forever. What a memory!

All things were going to be new, again! It was another major change in my life. I had a new home; I moved back to the Quad Cities where I had met

Jon. I was seeing old friends, looking for a new job, and living with the man of my dreams. I found a job and began playing lots of volleyball, while he played softball. Things were going great in our marriage. Until! It was time to expand our family. We were ready to have children. Because of Jon's age, he was eagerly awaiting the day to hear he was going to be a daddy. We tried for a couple of years without using any form of birth control, but nothing happened. We finally agreed to start going through the infertility testing process.

I tried different techniques: daily temperature to see what day I ovulated, standing on my head after sex, taking clomid, a biopsy of my uterus lining. I even went into the doctor's office right after having sex to make sure his sperm was reacting okay with my mucus, and dye treatment to see if my Fallopian tubes were open. The conclusion was to have laparoscopy surgery on my left Fallopian tube to open a blockage by my ovary, which was successful.

But they did say, "You have a tilted uterus and some endometriosis."

Month after month we continued to try and get pregnant, but still nothing! I was not pregnant. My sister, co-worker, and even my stepmother had more children.

Other women would tell me, "Oh I have a tilted uterus, and I got pregnant; or I had endometriosis, and I got pregnant."

These comments were very heartbreaking to hear from others who thought they were bringing me hope. But it was not! It would only upset me more and made the wound deeper. It was hard for me to go to baby showers, to see other women pregnant or experience Mother's Day. A day I never looked forward to celebrating.

I thought, '*What is wrong with me? Why am I not able to have children?*'

We still wanted hope so I went back to the doctor, but he could not find anything wrong with either one of us. He referred us to a hospital in another town. One of my co-workers went there and they told her she would have to adopt.

I was not ready to hear those words, "You will have to adopt." I became frustrated and refused to go saying, "No, I will not do that. I'm done! I have had enough heartache. I will do it myself."

I was in denial. I believed that there was nothing wrong with me and I always thought it was my husband's fault. This brought on even more stressful emotions in our marriage.

I still went through months of hoping and thinking, "This is the month I will get pregnant."

But nothing! I went through the emotional roller coaster ride month after month. NOTHING! There were times I honestly thought I was pregnant, but then Miss Flo would show up the same day someone would tell me they were pregnant. It would just crush me on the inside, and tears flowed uncontrollably. The sadness of not being able to give the man of my dreams a child was hard to accept each month. It made me, a barren woman, feel like I was not a whole person and a failure as a wife.

My sister had a new baby girl, and I became her godmother. After the baby dedication, the emotions were beyond my ability to manage and hit me extremely hard. I walked into the living room at my sister's house and saw my husband rocking this beautiful little baby girl in his arms. He looked so natural, comfortable, content, like he had become a perfect father. I ran to the back bedroom and just cried and cried.

I cried out to God, "Why Lord? Why? I do not understand!"

My sister came into the room trying to console me, but it did not work. She was even willing to be a surrogate mother for me, but her husband did not want her to do that.

Days passed, and I was able to pick myself back up again and keep pressing on. The months went by and then the years. The joy of holding a child in my arms never came. My emotions were beyond consoling. (If you have never been through this experience, you cannot understand the heartache of not being able to give the person you love a child.)

Hannah in the Bible could relate to how I was feeling. She cried out to God saying, *"… O Lord Almighty, if you will only look upon your servant's misery and remember me, and not forget your servant but give her a son, then I will give him to the Lord…"* 1 Samuel 1:10-11

One day I told my husband, "I am not happy. Something is missing," (Not knowing, at the time, it was Jesus missing in our lives.)

Jon's response was, "Do you think I am happy being with a woman who cannot give me a child?"

I was shocked by those words and devastated. It was as if he had just taken a dagger and pierced my heart and twisted it. I had hit rock bottom. I felt like I was no longer that precious lady he had fallen in love with years ago. Worthless and hopeless is how I felt.

"Where is the answer? What was I supposed to do?" kept playing in my head.

Chapter Three

THE SIN THAT CHANGED EVERYTHING

I was given the opportunity to go on a three-day mini cruise for the travel agency I was working for at the time. I was encouraged to go by my co-workers. So, I planned to take the trip to get some time away from the emotions I was dealing with daily.

I thought, *'This time away from my husband will be good for me emotionally. It will help me heal from those words he had spoken to me.'*

While on this cruise, I had a weird sensation/attraction toward a waiter that waited on us each meal. I was about to take matters into my own hands, not trusting in God's timing. I was in a very vulnerable state of mind. I was hoping this man could get me pregnant. We met one night, and things went just as I had planned. We had a one-night stand.

It brings me memories about how Sarah from the Bible did things her own way to get a son. She convinced Abraham to have relations with her maidservant, Hagar. Hagar did get pregnant with a son, Ishmael. However, my plan did not work. I did not get pregnant. It only brought heartache, just like with Sarah.

When I returned home, I could not forgive myself for what I had done, I only felt guilt for what I allowed to happen.

The thoughts kept going through my mind. '*What have I done?*'

I could no longer keep it from my husband about what happened. I finally got up the nerve to tell him. It was one of the hardest things I have ever had to do. He was shocked and deeply hurt by this newfound information I shared. He could not forgive my actions because I had defiled my body, and he no longer wanted any part of me. He wanted a divorce. The weekend fling, my adultery (sex outside of the marriage vows), ended our marriage of four and half years.

I thought to myself, '*Why did I have to move ahead of God? Why didn't I take my time and wait for His timing? I might not have missed what could have been in my future.*'

"Have you forgotten that your body is now the sacred temple of the Spirit of Holiness, who lives in you? You do not belong to yourself any longer, for the gift of God, the Holy Spirit, lives inside your sanctuary. You were God's expensive purchase, paid for with tears of blood, so, then, use your body to bring glory to God!" I Corinthians 6:19-20, TPT

I went to see a recommended counselor to help me get through that time in my life. The counselor told me to journal my feelings to get them out. I took the time to dig deep to let my feelings out as much as possible.

I remember writing in my journal, "Will I ever be able to find a man who will love me as a barren woman?"

My next major move was about to take place. I had no job, no friends, and no place to live just stepping out to the unknown, a new life. I ventured back to Florida to see if could run into the waiter on the cruise ship. Maybe I had a chance with him in my life. I scheduled myself on the same cruise, and we did get reconnected. It did not last long though. I realized that the relationship with him was not what I needed or wanted. I finally got settled in Florida by finding a place to live and made friends through the job I received as a cocktail waitress.

After a year and half, I got up the nerve to call my ex-husband to see how he was doing. I missed him. I did not prepare myself to hear what he had to say. He shared what I did not want to hear from him since we were not together anymore. He had just found out that he was expecting a child.

Ouch.

It was exactly how I felt: hurt. Because of my inability to have children, I still struggled emotionally to hear that from him. I never called him again. He had a new life, a new wife, and the child I could never give him.

Time went by and I got a new job working at a hotel as the front desk head shift-leader. I would periodically go out for drinks with a coworker. It was a Tuesday, $.25 draft night. We were sitting at the bar drinking when another co-worker and her boyfriend showed up. They introduced us to a gentleman named Scotty and two other ladies.

I talked to Scotty for a while. He had to leave for a second to use the restroom and asked me to wait. I waited for a little bit but then I had to leave because I had to work early the next morning.

About a week later, he contacted me at work. But the kicker was Scotty lived miles away in California, and I found out he was shorter than me. I remember standing next to a co-worker to see how tall he would be next to me, because the day I met him, I was sitting down the whole time and never realized he was that much shorter.

I thought, *'How is this going to work, him living there and me at the other end of the world it seems? How will we ever make this relationship work? Will I get over the height difference?'*

I was concerned about the inability to conceive children. So before considering starting a relationship, I asked him, "Would you be okay if I was never able to bear children? And do you mind that I am much taller than you?"

If he could not accept my barrenness, I did not want to hear from him ever again or attempt to start a relationship with him.

He agreed, "It's fine."

So, we continued the long-distance relationship for three months. I eventually moved to be closer to him. Another major move in my life with no friends, a new home, new culture, and no job. Though shortly after arriving in California, I found a job at a Travel Agency where I met new friends. I lived with my newfound love for about a year when the unexpected happened.

I bet you are thinking, "She finally got pregnant!"

Sorry to bust your bubble. No, that was not an unexpected event. We took a trip to Santa Barbara without anyone knowing that we went. Periodically, we would take weekend trips just to get away.

While at dinner, Scotty asked the server, "Is there a nice place to go in the area?"

The server said, "The pier."

So, after dinner, we took a long walk around the pier. We watched as men were fishing and breathed in the fresh cool breeze that swept over the pier from the ocean below.

Scotty kept repeating, "Watch out for the cracks!"

We slowly walked around to an area on the pier, an outlet where people fished. There was nobody in that area of the pier. It was darker, isolated, and a fearful feeling dwelled up within me.

He said, "Come over here and be closer to me."

I shook my head no, thinking, '*You are going to kill me. Nobody knows I am here with you.*'

But that was not what happened.

Pointing down at the crack between the wood planks, I said, "I will not cross that line."

He got down on his knee right there.

He asked, "Will you marry me?"

I was shocked, not expecting that at all.

I said, "Yes!"

The reason he kept saying watch out for the cracks was because he did not want me to drop the engagement ring into the ocean by accident.

One weekend while we were visiting my sister, she was showing me the new diamond ring her husband had just given her, and I dropped the ring right into my glass of milk while I was looking at it.

I gasped, "Oh no!" I was so embarrassed.

Well, we planned to get married that next Valentine's Day. It was a small wedding with friends and family members. It was a crazy busy day to get married in Las Vegas, especially at the hotel where our wedding took place. Every wedding lasted less than 10 minutes, in and out quickly. I was so nervous that I was shaking and had a tough time getting the ring on my finger.

We continued our married life as any normal marriage would be lived. Back to our work life and living as a newly married couple. Sharing some new memories with family and friends. We got introduced to a network marketing business that began to develop at a slow pace. But we enjoyed being around the positive environment.

Chapter Four

A FRESH START

On the twelfth of March, at a Sunday morning business conference church service, a lady was sharing her testimony about how she came to know the Lord, and how He had changed her life forever. She gave everyone present the opportunity to receive Jesus as their Lord and Savior. My heart was racing and burning within to walk forward but I was afraid to make that move down the aisle.

I kept pondering, '*What will the other people think? I do not want people staring at me. Am I doing the right thing? How could this Jesus love an unworthy sinner like me? I am not good enough. Maybe when I get my life in order, then maybe I will do it.*'

I could not take the burning desire inside me away any longer and made the move to the front of the stage where the lady was speaking. We prayed the sinner's prayer admitting our sins and receiving forgiveness; believing that Jesus died on the cross and rose again to make it possible to live in communion with God; and choosing to walk in His footsteps.

This experience totally changed my perspective on who God is; His love is unconditional, no matter what I may have done in the past. I cried with joy in my heart to know that someone loved me for who I was with my unchangeable mistake I made and all my flaws.

The Bible says, "*…For if you publicly declare with your mouth Jesus is Lord and believe in your heart that God raised Him from the dead, you will experience salvation.*

The heart that believes in Him receives the gift of righteousness of God--and the mouth confesses, resulting in salvation." Romans 10:9-10, TPT

"Therefore, if anyone is in Christ, he is a new creation. The old has gone, the new has come." 2 Corinthians 5:17

Now forgiven of all my past, present, and any future sins, I began growing in my faith with the help of attending different bible studies.

Scotty walked forward to receive Jesus Christ at another business conference we attended in August of the same year.

The Bible was correct in saying that, *"Believe in the Lord Jesus and you and your household will be saved." Acts 16:31*

We had been attending a church for a while and I felt it was time to get baptized. I was ready. On the day the church announced they would be having baptismal class, I had to refrain from jumping out of my seat and saying, "I want to do it! Baptize me! Baptize me!"

We attended the class and were baptized on the eighth of October, a date I will never forget. We shared our testimony in front of everyone present. I cried through my testimony because I was so thankful for what Jesus had done for me, and my emotions were heightened as I felt the overwhelming power of the Holy Spirit within me.

After that day, my hunger grew to be in God's Word daily, and I eventually attended an in-depth discipleship week of training. While I was at this training in August of the next year, I was given the bible study, *Experiencing God,* by Henry Blackaby. Drawn to this bible study like no other, I went through the study by myself.

By the end of the study, I could sense God saying, *"I want you to lead this study."* (Blackaby, 1990, p. 264)

I stepped out in faith scared to death. I was a new believer and did not understand much of the Bible. Two ladies responded to the invitations to do the study, and we all grew closer to God and each other. It was amazing. I was also given the privilege to go through the study with my neighbor.

I had taken one of the spiritual gifts tests through my church, and a pastor from my church recommended that I help aid in organizing the women's ministry bible study which met weekly. I agreed and stepped out in faith again believing this was what God wanted me to do. I enjoyed the new opportunity given to me to work with women. It was a true blessing. My focus was on leading women to Christ, but Scotty had a different focus. He wanted to have children.

I thought, '*No! I do not want to go through the struggle of trying again. How can I?*' I still hurt from the former situation of trying to have children and I was not ready to face more pain.

I prayed, "Lord, could you give me a child without going through the emotional pain again?"

I sensed God responding through the *Experiencing God* study "I really want to, but if I were to put you into that kind of assignment, you would never be able to handle it. You are not ready." (Blackaby, 1990, p. 192)

WOW!!! He was right. I did need more healing to take place.

But that journey was only beginning.

I decided to attend an infertility bible study group to deal with the issue of my barrenness. Through the group, I was able to let go of the past hurts, but I was struggling with the fear of having a child.

I looked up the word 'Afraid' in the concordance at the back of my Bible and this was the conversation I sensed I had with God.

God: Genesis 26:24, *"Do not be afraid, for I am with you; I will increase the number of your descendants for the sake of my servant Abraham."*

Me: I need to trust and believe that God will bless me with a child. Psalm 56:3, *"When I am afraid, I will trust you."* Lord, help me to trust You and believe that what You are saying to me is true.

God: Matthew 8:26, *"…You of little faith, why are you afraid?"*

Me: "I am afraid of being a good mother, afraid of possibly hurting the child like my mother did me, and afraid of gaining weight."

Voice in my head (Holy Spirit) said, "It will be okay!" Mark 5:36, *"Don't be afraid, just believe."*

I was overwhelmed by how God was speaking to me.

I responded by singing the song by Crystal Lewis: "I believe in You, and I put my trust in You. Though I cannot see You with my eyes, deep in my heart Your presence I find. Lord, I believe."

By admitting and understanding my fears, I found the courage to research methods on how to conceive a child.

During bible study time again, I came across this statement, "God wants you to depend on Him-not a method or program." (Blackaby, 1990, p. 136)

I thought, *'Is God testing me?'* If He was, I wanted to make sure not to let any new method be more important than Him.

More time passed and it was 2001. The leader of the infertility class encouraged me to make a doctor appointment. The doctor found out that I had a cyst on my left ovary and watched it for three months putting me on menopause medication to shrink the cyst. It did not work, and I scheduled surgery to remove it.

During consultation after the surgery, the doctor said that I had severe endometriosis: an often-serious disorder in which the lining of the uterus grows outside of the uterus. She removed what she could. There was nothing more she could do. She referred us to go to an IVF clinic or consider adoption.

I thought, '*Oh no! Not the adoption word again.*'

I finally had to accept the fact that I was not going to have a child physically and adoption was the one way that I could accomplish the goal. I had to trust God to make the final decision on which child would be in our life.

My thought through the adoption process was, '*If every person had to go through the adoption process, possibly fewer children would be born.*'

It felt like an interrogation. The house had to be perfect. We had to put a bio together on each of us and put a family portfolio together in hopes that an expecting mom would like what she saw. Finally in April of 2003, we were placed on an adoption waiting list as available adoptive parents.

Chapter Five

THE BLESSING FROM GOD

It was a normal day at work. I tried not to think about the waiting process and just try to live life as usual. One day, unexpectedly, a co-worker said, "I know of a 14-year-old that just got pregnant and is not sure what she will do with the baby. I mentioned to her that you were trying to adopt. You know who this teen is."

I could not think of any teen that was pregnant. A couple of days later a voice in my head (Holy Spirit) said, "Ashley!" Then days later I saw her walking by the classroom at church and sure enough, it was her. Through the *Experience God* study, I had an experience I will never forget. The conversations I sensed I was having with God throughout the study went like this:

God: "The time God comes to me is the time for me to respond. I need to begin adjusting my life to Him. I may need to prepare for what He is about to do through me." (Blackaby, 1990, p. 85)

Me: "Lord, right now I pray for answers about this teen. I feel You, God, have revealed to me who she is before really knowing. I believe that You have come to me through my coworkers. I am willing to take this child if the possibility becomes available. I pray that You will help me be prepared for what may lie ahead."

Study five days later: "Remain in a close relationship with Him so I can always hear His voice when He wants to speak to me. When God accomplishes His purpose in His way through me, people will come to know God. They will recognize that what happened, can be explained only by God. He will get the glory to Himself." (Blackaby, 1990, p. 101)

Me: "I am going to go to God and clarify what I am absolutely convinced He is saying to me. Then I am going to proceed and watch to see how God affirms it." (Blackaby, 1990, p. 102)

Lord, are You saying to me that Ashley wants us to possibly be the parents for her child? I pray for wisdom for all parties involved and believe that You will get the glory for what is about to happen, because only You could have done this wonderful thing. Amen.

Six days later in my time with the Lord, the study said, "I must dismiss any selfish or fleshly desires of my own. As I start to pray, the Spirit of God starts to touch my heart and cause me to pray in the direction of God's will." (Blackaby, 1990, p. 109)

Me: "Lord, I do pray for this situation with Ashley. Help me to dismiss any selfish desires and pray for what is best for her and her child. I want Your will, Lord. If it is Your will that we bring up this child in our home, then help us to have a wonderful relationship with all family members involved."

The very next day, Ashley and her mom called me into a room at church to talk in private. I held my emotions together at the meeting and just busted into tears afterwards. It was starting to happen just as God said. Ashley wanted to meet Scotty and me for an interview to see if she would feel comfortable with us being the parents to her child. We scheduled to meet Saturday at our home. It was a stretch, because we said in our adoption process, we would never allow the birthmother to know where we lived.

The Saturday meeting arrived and went well. We found out that her grandmother also had the same color hair as mine when she was younger and the birthfather was part Filipino, like Scotty. This was becoming a perfect match. Ashley was willing to consider adoption if she could see the baby anytime she wanted. We agreed and gave Ashley the adoption agency's contact information with which we were working.

I asked Ashley that day, "What is one thing you have always wanted, but could not have?" I asked this because having a child is one thing I was never able to have.

Ashley replied, "A kitten."

Her mother finally agreed for Ashley to have a kitten.

A week later, Scotty and I went to a prayer meeting. It was stirring in my heart to share what was happening. That morning my prayer was "increase my faith." I got up the nerve to share with a group of adults that we may become parents soon. I shared my story, and the group felt led to lay hands directly on us and pray. I found out later that at the exact same time, Ashley was sharing her testimony with the High School Church Group. They also laid hands directly on her for prayer.

Ashley called me days later and asked me to think about this question, "Since I did not have any prenatal care, would you still be willing to take the baby if he/she was deformed?"

I was sensing in my spirit that God already wanted us to be the parents. I knew in my heart the answer was YES but did not say anything yet. We scheduled Wednesday night to meet for prayer and to share our answers. The day came with great anticipation. Upon arrival, there were four families in the room besides us and Ashley's family. I was overwhelmed with what was about to happen. I waited so many years to hear that I was going to be a mommy. My heart was beating, hands sweating, and mind racing.

I thought to myself, '*What is Ashley going to say? How am I going to respond if the answer is Yes or if it is No? Will this be another day that will forever change my life?*' With excitement in her voice, Ashley said, "Yes, I want you to be the parents to my child."

I covered my face to hide the tears of joy. I responded with, "Yes, we will be the parents of your child and Benjamin will be the boy's name or Brealynn for the girl's name."

One of the ladies said the baby's initials needed to be BLT. We found out that Ashley's dad's middle name was Lee, and her mother's middle name was Lynn. Since we already had Lynn in the girl's first name, we were going to use both mine and Ashley's middle name as her middle name, Mae.

Ashley wasn't scheduled to deliver for three more weeks. Since we did not have baby things, a friend of mine agreed to help me register at a department store. Upon arriving in the parking lot, we got the call that the baby was coming sooner than expected. So, we just grabbed quick items that I would need right away.

Everyone present at the delivery was exhausted. I had the privilege to see the whole delivery and the opportunity to cut the umbilical cord. Baby boy Benjamin Lee arrived at 3:43 am three days after being told we would be parents.

We had a ceremony in the hospital room the next day, and Ashley placed her birth-son in my arms. Another emotional day! As newly excited parents, we took Benjamin home to be our son. It had been sixteen long years waiting for this day to occur.

Like Abraham with Sarah, waiting until the time was exactly right to bring Isaac into the world, God's timing is always best.

Ashley's family came over to help plan a baby shower. We needed supplies for this new addition to the family. While Scotty was out running errands, he brought home two kittens, with adoption papers, to give to Ashley. Not one, but two. They were the cutest kittens. A later story will reveal the effects these kittens had on the family, but for now just know they were a joyful addition to Ashley's family.

I started to settle into my changed life as a new mom. One day I was on the couch just holding my new baby boy in my arms still in shock that this had truly happened. I just held him crying and thanking God for turning a tough situation into something beautiful. Oh, the joy of being a mother. I never wanted to let this moment slip away. That was another emotional moment and day.

God is faithful in keeping His promises and can work miracles in different situations. He gets all the praise and glory for what has happened in my life. He had done a work on me and my circumstance. God never ceases to amaze me.

"I prayed for this child, and the Lord has granted me what I asked of Him."
I Samuel 1:27a

About a week later, it was late at night, and Ashley called wanting to see Benjamin. I was more than happy to have her, and her mother came over never wanting to prevent Ashley from ever seeing her birth child. She was having a challenging time wondering if she had made the right decision. After leaving that day, she felt more confident about her decision. We were considered one big family. They visited often and watched Benjamin during the day while I went back to work.

Benjamin started having health issues. I wondered, *'What could possibly be wrong?'* He would come home from Ashley's parent's house with sniffles then get better at our house. We could not understand what was causing this sickness. They thought it could be allergies to something, but not sure what.

Well, Ashley's family moved to Utah, because of her dad's job transfer. Benjamin's health seemed to improve overnight. On one thanksgiving, while visiting them in Utah, we come to realize what was causing Benjamin's health issues. Remember the kittens? Those cute cuddly kittens were now fully grown cats that had the run of the house. Benjamin would play on the floor with his toys. Over a brief period, we noticed that his

31

breathing became heavy. He was having an allergic reaction to the cat-dander.

His breathing got so bad that we had to check into a hotel instead of staying with the family. Because of the health concerns and his allergies, we had to cut back on how often we could see them.

Chapter Six

HEALING THE HEART

About three years later, I was introduced to a college course online. It was recommended as something that could help me heal from things in my past. My experience through this course was: WOW is all I can say!

While reading one of the assigned readings, *Blessings or Curses: You Can Choose*, by Derek Prince, I prayed for deliverance from generational sins and curses such as: teenage pregnancy, adultery, divorce, abortion, illnesses, and lack of income. I did not feel or see any difference from praying through these prayers. I just trusted that God had healed me from these generational curses and sins.

I started praying through whatever negative expectation or inner vow I made with myself that came to mind, such as how I would say, "I'm not good enough," because I did not value myself. Even though my dad encouraged me to get my job with the airlines, he used to say repeatedly, "You will never amount to anything." And since I experienced my siblings having teenage pregnancies, I told myself as a young teen, "I don't want to get pregnant."

I must set aside these thoughts daily to keep my mind free from negativity.

The Bible says in *Philippians 4:8*, *"...whatever is true, whatever is noble, whatever is right, whatever is pure, whatever is lovely, whatever is admirable--if anything is excellent or praiseworthy--think about such things,"*

The next book on the reading assignment was *You Can Be Emotionally Free*, by Rita Bennett. This was truly an emotional ride. I had to deal with issues that I have never had to really face before. I tucked them down inside.

One night, I had a dream that went like this:

Dream

I saw a green lizard-like thing trying to jump on my bed. I kicked it off. I also tried to pick up the lizard, and it bit my hand. I thought, *'I better go put peroxide on it to make sure it does not get infected.'* As I was pouring the peroxide on my hand, the whole top layer of my skin came off, and I then received a noticeably big open wound. I was determined to destroy this lizard.

Since the light was so dim, it was hard for me to see anything. I saw it moving and went for it. I picked up the lizard by the tail and tried stuffing it into a jar, but it was too big. Then I woke up.

My Interpretation

I believed that I still had a wound I had not found yet, and that when I found it, it would open and be painful. But I would be determined to deal with it. It was my divorce from my first husband, Jon. I never wanted to face the fact that I was the one that caused the divorce by committing adultery, which was eighteen years before, in 1990. I had always said it was because of my infertility, essentially blaming him.

I decided to bring closure to this pain in my past and wrote Jon an apology. I was scared to send the letter, but I did. I thought, *'Will he get the letter? How will he respond to it? Will I hear back from him?'* Two weeks of uneasiness ended when the letter was non-deliverable to the wrong address.

What an emotional process! I was still very emotional about all of it but was unable to cry. Here is a dialogue I sensed I was having with God.

Me: Lord, why is it so hard for me to cry?

God: My child, when you were growing up, your earthly father did not like to have you cry. He was struggling with his own hurts and every time you would cry it reminded him of his sad times in life. He loved you just like I love you. He just did not know how to express it. As a child, he did not receive the affection that he needed. Without someone showing him, it is difficult for him to know how to show it. He tried his best to bring you up in a loving home the best he knew how. Forgive him for how he may have hurt you.

Me: Jesus, please tell my dad (who passed away) these words, "Dad, I love you. I forgive you. You did the best you knew how. Jesus is healing me from hurtful memories. Please forgive me too if I have wronged you in any way. I will not hold it against you anymore. I set you free and I set myself free." Thank you, Jesus, for letting my daddy know!

That night I just bawled until my eyes hurt. I sensed God said to me: "Julie, just remember that I am the one doing all the healing, and that I get all the glory in any progress in people's lives. Right now, you still need more confidence in what you are learning. I will give you that confidence. Keep moving forward.

Be obedient to Me, and I will lead you in the way everlasting. Pass on the knowledge you are receiving with others so that they too can heal.

Then, In January of 2009, I felt physically attacked. I was having pain in my left side ovaries area. When I saw the doctor, they did an ultrasound and noticed that I had a large cyst that was cloudy. I mentioned having a hysterectomy, and they did not hesitate to do it. I wonder if they knew something but were not sharing it with me.

The day I had my hysterectomy the doctor found out that my left kidney was smaller and had issues. They put a stent in to open my ureter. Eventually, I had to have my left kidney removed because the ureter closed, and infection began to affect my kidney. At the same time, I was dealing with my health issues, Scotty was going through thyroid cancer. I felt that the evil one was working overtime trying to discourage me.

But I was determined to keep going. I had Jesus on my side. He has already won the battle! *'May God give me wisdom and reassurance in my dreams that everything is going to be okay!'*

Through all of this, I still struggled with Trust. So, I looked up verses that had trust in it. Below are the verses I read.

Bible Meditation Concerning Trust

Exodus 14:31 – When people see God's power at work, then they will fear the Lord and put their trust in Him.

Psalm 9:10 – God will never leave me no matter what I face.

Psalm 56:3-4 - When I am afraid, I will trust in You.

Psalm 62:8 – Trust in God always, pour out my heart to Him for He is my refuge.

Isaiah 8:17 – Be willing to wait and accept the Lord's timing, not mine.

Isaiah 26:4 - Trust in the Lord forever, for the Lord, the Lord, is the Rock eternal.

Romans 15:13 - May the God of hope fill me with all joy and peace as I trust in Him; so that I may overflow with hope by the power of the Holy Spirit.

These biblical truths helped set me free to put more trust in the Lord and try not to carry the burden on my own. He loves me unconditionally and will never leave me nor forsake me. The verse that helped me the most during this time of meditation was:

May the God of hope fill me with all joy and peace as I trust in Him; so that I may overflow with hope by the power of the Holy Spirit. Romans 15:13

I made my Memorial Stone to be a penny! In God I trust! A Memorial Stone is something that reminds me of God and Him working in my life.

Two days later, I began seeing pennies in the strangest of places. I had just finished putting Benjamin down for bed and getting Scotty out the door for work – he worked nights. I went to my bedroom to get ready for bed. In the middle of my bed was a penny on top of the quilt. How it got there only God knows. I just prayed, "Thank You God that I can trust in You."

The next day, I had to have Benjamin's aunt take him to school so I could go to my doctor's appointment. I had to put his car seat in her car. As I moved things around, I saw another penny. "Thank You Lord that I can trust You to take care of my son and me."

After the doctor's appointment, Scotty and I went to the store to get things we needed. As I was walking out of the door, there was a penny on the ground. "Thank You Lord that I can trust You to supply our needs."

I decided I was going to start collecting the pennies that I saw in strange places like those I mentioned as reminders of what God can and will do for me.

I can trust in the Lord. I am healed, but I will keep checking with the Holy Spirit to reveal any more areas to heal.

Chapter Seven

COUNSELED BY GOD

Once I signed up for the next course, *Counseled by God,* by Mark Virkler and Patti Virkler, I started feeling every emotion of depression, anger, fear, and guilt, all of which the course discussed without my even knowing beforehand. God wanted me to experience these emotions so that I would be able to help someone else to overcome them.

During that time, Jon tried contacting me via Facebook. It brought back the guilt of what I had done. I thought, '*Has he forgiven me? Is he still married?*" I did not respond to him, but memories of him kept coming to me over the next two weeks.

Then there came a moment where I needed to get my password and every clue was about him. Scotty listened to music and the songs would bring back memories of Jon. I determined Jon must have been placed back into my life for more healing.

Scotty saw that Jon tried to contact me via Facebook and then Scotty took over my Facebook page. That caused me to get incredibly angry and bitter toward him. He must have feared that I was going to talk with Jon again, and this way he could check my Facebook.

The four different emotions that I had to face brought me a healing I did not expect.

First Emotion: Depression

I had to deal with my depression. I was struggling because my privacy no longer was mine. This is what I asked the Lord. "Lord, help snap me out of this mood. I have been like this way too long now. Help me focus on the right things. God, guide this day. May Your joy fill my spirit! Please! I need to laugh again. Help me laugh again."

This is what I sensed the Lord was saying to me. "Julie, a strong person knows how to keep their life in order. Even with the tears in their eyes, they still manage to say, 'I am okay!' with a smile. I AM a good God. Change is coming. I have seen your sadness and said, 'Hard times are over.' So, smile. Now shall I tell you the way to real pleasure? I call it the way of surrender. It is a straight and narrow path, but it does lead to pleasure. Surrender your desires each one of them to Me! Yield every desire to My Spirit, and you will find joy. Surprises await you. Your problem is lack of pleasure, real pleasure."

I needed to learn that true pleasure is found in the Lord.

Second Emotion: Anger

I had another dream. One evening, Scotty turned on the TV, and it was very loud. I went to turn it off because Benjamin did not need to be watching a completely defaced person on the screen with only their right eye showing. I said, "You cannot be watching this." I went to turn it off but then Scotty said, "No, leave it on." I was getting angry. Scotty was busy fixing something, and I walked to Benjamin's bedroom to find his bed had been moved away from the wall, which was strange. Then I headed to my bedroom. I saw that the blankets and sheets were a mess on the bed. I said to myself, "I hate you!" Scotty came back to the bedroom, looked in the room, and left by slamming the door shut. I woke up truly angry inside. I rebuked the anger in the name of Jesus and asked God to fill me with His love.

"What does this mean, Lord?" I asked.

I sensed that He said, "Julie, one of the areas that I needed to show you is your anger. You need to get it under control. I have told you these things so that you can have peace. You are destined to be a compassionate deliverer and you will have healing gifts to share. As you share them, you will spare much of the heartache you have known. Now will you accept My gifts and please stop mouthing off all kinds of nonsense? Let Us dry those tears. You will need unclouded vision to enter the new door I AM now opening. I have more to tell you, but you are too young to bear it now."

Third Emotion: Fear

I was afraid of the unknown.

This is what I sensed God said to me, "Julie, why have I been leading you through this obstacle course of pressured events? I have allowed them for one practical reason: to deliver you from fear for the last time. More you are coming to trust Me; less and less you are fearing the future. Every time those threats have reared their silly heads, I have repeatedly shown you My power to bring them to nothing. And I AM building an inner peace in you at the same time. Julie, there are still areas We both want to see healed, but those little pockets of pain have been inside you a long time. And to remove them all at once would be unwise. It requires a certain pace and process. To heal all at once would deny you the opportunity to gain experience and to become a compassionate deliverer.

Put your hand in Mine and your heart in tune with My Spirit, and you will see those things you want materialize in an amazing way. I AM teaching you to become effective in believing. Receive the teaching of My divine Spirit. This is the time in your life in which you must nail down every fact and figure and call upon every resource within you to get specific plans off the ground.

You must narrow your focus and commit to what is most important to you, and the pieces will fall into place with the guidance of the Holy Spirit.

Do not be concerned with what is far ahead. Just take one step at a time. I AM leading you with My divine Spirit and love. What happens within you is what I AM concerned about."

Fourth Emotion: Guilt

I had to face the guilt of what I did in the past.

This is what I felt God was telling me. "Julie, about those feelings of guilt… forgiven. While you are making choices, choose to forgive yourself. Self-inflicted punishment can do nothing to alter the past. So, will you simply enjoy My love and go on sharing it with others. I have set before you an open door. Remembering this will spare you further stress.

Cease all remorse and stop trying to analyze your recent blunders. Forgiven. I simply want to help you put it to better use. Look only where I instruct you to look and trust Me. Learn the peace that defies reason. I will give you an unearthly calm that no storm, no fiery furnace, and no contradiction can challenge if you will look only to Me. But again—you MUST look only at Me. I will lead you in the way you should go, and I will contend with every enemy. Have I not recently told you this? No longer linger between two opinions. Pursue peace and I will perfect your path!"

God has healed me of all these issues and has brought me peace.

I believed God was saying, "Julie, I tell you that you are heading into a new level of Spiritual manifesting in your life. Questions in your mind settled by reading and understanding the Scripture. As you read it, ask Me for My Spirit to guide you, it will become clear to you. The Holy Spirit will reveal its meaning to you. I AM educating you for things to come and for patience to manage what you are facing now. Reading the Holy Scriptures requires focus. Obedience is a consistent event. Pray for every action. Your inner peace is a signal to help guide you, and the Holy Spirit always confirms His guidance."

Over the twelve weeks of the course, I experienced healing take place in my heart and my life. I was at more peace than I had ever been in my life. I thank my Heavenly Father for reaching down and touching my life with His healing power, love, and compassion.

From that point on, I tried to allow God to guide my footsteps. I felt led to go back to a different college to work on my master's degree because the one I was attending did not offer accreditation.

Chapter Eight

LIVING IN EXPECTATION

Going back to 2015, new things had developed in my life that were causing drastic changes again. Right after going through the *Experiencing God* study, I went into a deep depression for a good month and half. I was nervous about looking for a job because I had not worked for the last seven years and was preparing to graduate from college. With God's help, I was able to overcome this depression, and what happened next was unimaginable.

I thought, *'The first place to start looking for a job is where Benjamin is going to go to Junior High.'*

I looked for an internship position at his school as a school counselor. His school did not have any openings, but the gentleman referred me to two other schools that did have openings for an intern. Both head counselors met with me on the same day.

The first school, a high school, accepted me with open arms and no questions asked. I went to the next school, an elementary school, and I was there for only ten minutes. They needed special paperwork for the internship. Due to the winter weather storm that closed the university I was attending, I found out days later that my degree did not offer an internship. And on that same day, I lost the diamond out of my wedding ring. I was devastated and stressed for four days. I could not eat and could feel it in my neck and stomach.

At the high school where I was earlier accepted, I wondered how I was going to tell them that I did not qualify for an internship. The school counselor was a Christian, which made it easier to tell her. She accepted me with open arms.

The next day, I had to meet the counselor at the high school at 6:45 am. At 6:10 am, I could not find the car keys. I checked my purse three times, nothing. Finally, I found the spare keys, and made it to the high school on time.

After school was over, I started driving home and looked down at the keys in the ignition. They were the keys I had not been able to find that morning. I thought, *'What the heck! How did these keys get into my purse when they were not there this morning?'* Guess what? The experience of getting to that high school only got better.

The next day, I got a text from the school counselor that said, "Meet me at the elementary school." It was for that same morning. I had an idea of where to go but still got lost. I stopped for directions at a gas station. The gas attendant was not sure where the elementary school was either, but two children walked into the store. The children just happened to attend the school. I went outside and knocked on their mother's car door for directions and was able to find the school.

That night Benjamín was upset that I was not taking him to school or picking him up. I had not worked the whole time he had been in school. This was an adjustment he was not taking well. It made me feel terrible that I could not be there for my son like I had been over the last seven years. So, the next day, I took him to school, but had to drop him off early. I still needed to get gas in the car. As I was waiting patiently for a pump to become available, a gentleman cut right in front of me in line. I could not believe what had just happened. *'This is going to delay me from getting to work on time,'* I thought.

46

Finally, I was off to work. Taking a new way to get to work, I passed a paved road next to a different elementary school, which I needed to take, and turned around to take that road. I made it to work just on time.

The next morning, Benjamin wanted French toast for breakfast, which was time consuming to make, but I agreed. As I was gathering things to make the French toast, I looked down on the floor and next to the kitchen sink lay my diamond! I placed the diamond back into my ring.

I was so excited; I ran to tell Benjamin, "Guess what? I found my diamond."

I went back out into the kitchen to continue preparing the French toast, looked down, and the diamond was missing again.

I thought, '*Oh no! Where could it have gone? I cannot believe it just fell out again.*' I opened the refrigerator, and there on the shelf was the diamond. I went out into the garage to find a pair of pliers to tighten the diamond into place.

"There, that should hold it in place," I said.

It was time to leave for school. I still had time to get to work, so I thought. On the way, there was an accident that caused traffic for miles bumper to bumper. I had nowhere to go, but sat there wondering, '*Why is it so hard for me to get to this high school every day? Am I supposed to be there? Is this my donkey in the road preventing me from going forward described in the Bible?*'

After dropping Benjamin off at his school early again the next day, I decided to take the route I took the week before. However, I made a mistake and turned a street too early and drove for about two miles before coming to a dead end.

Turning around and heading back, I decided to take another street which led to another dead end. By that time, I was furious and yelling at the top of my lungs, "What the *#####*?" Ready to pull my hair out, I almost backed into a 12-inch cement wall. Finally, I was on the street I was supposed to take in the first place. At that point I was driving like a mad woman trying to get to the high school on time. I came to the paved road that I had passed the week before, but this time it was a dirt road, and the elementary school was nowhere to be found.

I thought, '*Oh, am I going crazy? What else could go wrong this morning? This is so ridiculous.*'

I got to the school 5 minutes late and had to park all the way to the end of the parking lot. I had an exceedingly long walk to the counselor's building. I keep thinking to myself, '*Is this the donkey in the road saying do not go there, or is this some serious opposition because I am headed in the right direction?*'

"*Wait for the Lord; be strong and take heart and wait for the Lord.*" Psalm 27:14

I shared how hard it was to get to school on time with the school counselor I was working alongside. She was very gracious, helpful, and flexible with my schedule to work around Benjamin's school hours. After that, I continued to help at the high school for two more months until graduation day and had no more difficulties in getting to the school. I was relieved not to have any more crazy experiences.

Chapter Nine

THE OPEN DOOR

After graduating and with the internship over, I had to start looking for a job. Doors kept closing; I was either overqualified or needed more education. I was getting very discouraged and feeling like a complete failure.

I thought, *'What am I going to do? This master's degree is getting me nowhere.'* Scotty was getting concerned as well.

What happened next, I was not expecting either!

I went to the post office and ran into a friend who I had not seen in a long time.

My friend asked, "Are you working for such and such ministry?"

I said, "No." and never thought anymore about it.

Well, three days later, I ran into the bookkeeper from that ministry at the department store. She was telling me how they had expanded and just hired a case manager. I thought to myself, *'Darn, I just missed the opportunity to apply.'* Then two days later, I ran into the bookkeeper again at a home supply store.

I said to her, "If I run into you again, I am supposed to go to the ministry for some reason."

I was still getting daily pressure from Scotty to find a job. It made me feel worthless. I would just sit there not saying a word. What could I have said?

After the event with the bookkeeper, a friend of mine asked, "Why do you have a key tied to your Bible?"

I said, "I will look up the exact wording of what it means when I get home and share next time we met."

I went to look up the information in my past sermon notes from church. The notes written down were "Take the key and unlock the door of forgiveness." The reason I had the key on my Bible was to remind me to forgive others and not lock them in a cage. I kept reading my sermon notes and I sensed God said, "I will be with you and qualify you for it."

A second later, I received a text from another friend.

She asked, "Did you receive the email that the ministry is hiring? I recommended you for the job."

I replied, "No, but I will contact them, and thank you."

Well instantly, I contacted another friend, who taught classes there. Shocking news came. She no longer worked there, and it was her position that was open. She still encouraged me to apply.

So, I sent the executive director my resume and I received a phone interview the following week, since my family was going on vacation. I had to wait three days for the decision on whom he would hire. I knew deep down in my heart that God had opened the door for me to get the job and position. I had asked, had been looking for, and now had found it.

"Ask and it will be given to you; seek and you will find; knock and the door will be opened to you." Matthew 7:7

Patiently I waited. The phone call came. I expected the answer to whom he had hired would be me.

The Executive Director said, "Yes, you are hired for the position."

I was so excited and learned I would start that next Monday with three days of training. At the first staff meeting, I introduced myself and shared how I came to get the position at the Ministry. Then everyone else introduced themselves, and how they became part of the ministry.

After everyone had finished sharing, one of the staff members said, "The Holy Spirit was present at this staff meeting. The team is now complete."

I felt welcomed and accepted. I knew I was where I was supposed to be for the time being.

Chapter Ten

WHO KNEW

As time goes on, life situations can catch you by surprise.

I had started working for the ministry as a parent facilitator and began to struggle with staying there. It was a big adjustment to the lifestyle of the clientele I helped. The new job also affected my home life. I did not understand how women can work a full-time job, be a full-time mom, and be a full-time homemaker.

Something had to give. Dinner-making stopped happening, I was unable to help in Benjamin's classroom anymore, and work got the best of me. Family vacations happened less and less. Then on one of our few vacations, I noticed something inappropriate on Scotty's phone. Over the years of marriage, I had encountered it but had been in denial that he was looking at those things. The visual I saw made the denial reality. I was hurt, upset, and angry. *".... and you may be sure that your sin will find you out." Numbers 32:23b*

I thought, *'What am I going to do with this newfound information?'*

I went to my pastor at the time and poured out my heart in tears in front of him and Scotty. The pastor mentioned going to counseling. I scheduled an appointment to meet with a couple that helped with struggling marriages. We only met once and never met again because the couple's health was not good. I just tried to live with the fact that he was doing this throughout our whole marriage.

God sometimes brings things full circle and gives second chances. It was about two years later, 2017, and I had a very heavy burden to contact my first husband, Jon. I sensed that there was something wrong with him. He might have been having health issues. The only way I knew how to contact him was via Facebook. I set up a new Facebook account with just the two of us to communicate. When we connected, I asked if he was having any health issues.

He said, "No, but my dad is going to have open heart surgery soon."

I said, "I must be needing to pray for your dad."

I asked him if he had forgiven me for what I had done. The area of forgiveness I never expected to receive happened. It was forgiveness that helped free and heal me even more.

The situation with Scotty continued to escalate until I decided I could not live with him anymore. I wanted to file for divorce. It was hard because I also knew it would affect Benjamin.

I thought, '*How is he going to get through this*?' They say that children are more resilient, but I did not want to hurt him.

My life was not the same after that. I went through the *Experiencing God* study again knowing that God would radically change my life somehow, but not knowing how yet.

Well during the study, I read "*Faith used powerfully in Abraham for when he put it to the test, he offered up Isaac. Even though he received God's promises of descendants, he was willing to offer up his only son!*" Hebrews 11:17 TPT.

I thought, '*Is it so ironic that my experience with having children started with Abraham and now twenty years later his name appears in my life again?*'

I sensed that God was asking me to sacrifice my son by giving him up, like He asked Abraham to do with his son, Issac.

I thought, '*How could I do this?*'

For the next four months, I struggled with the thought of letting my son go. As a reminder that I was going in the right direction, I experienced different events in my life. On one such time, I was collaborating with an intern who sat in my office for hours at work, named none other than *Abraham*!

The time was coming for me to tell my son about moving back to Illinois and that I was going to leave him with his dad. I was scared to let him know.

One day, on our way to his school, I got up the nerve to share with him what was going to happen. His reaction was unforeseen. He shared that he would be fine with it. I was relieved to know that he would be okay with staying. I still was not convinced I was doing the right thing.

That weekend I attended a retreat called *That Was Then, This is Now.* I needed confirmation to keep moving forward. On Saturday night during worship and prayer time, the speaker spoke out about what God was either placing on her heart or giving her visually when she prayed.

She shared, "I see a man, no it is a son, standing in the driveway waving good-bye, and that you can trust God to take care of him."

That hit my heart. I went up to her afterwards and asked, "Do you ever remember what you say when you pray?"

She responded "Sometimes."

I asked, "Do you remember the one about the son?"

She said, "Yes, you have to let him go."

I was overwhelmed to the point of tears.

The next day, we had to draw a line in the sand next to a cross and walk over it into a new walk with the Lord. It was my turn to go.

I knelt at the cross, and in my mind, I placed Benjamin on the altar for God to take care of him. It was another emotional time of letting go. The Lord had given me my son, and now I was giving him to the Lord. Same as in Hannah's prayer.

O Lord Almighty, if you will only look upon your servant's misery and remember me, and not forget your servant but give her a son, then I will give him to the Lord... 1 Samuel 1:10-11.

After I stepped over the line, the speaker that prayed over me said, "All I see are a lot of question marks ???"

As a reminder of what had just happened, I walked over to a table that had watches on it. I spotted one that was unique. It was a necklace with a saying, "Faith makes things possible, not easy." I chose that watch to be my reminder of God taking care of my son.

For the next forty days my goal was to meditate on different versions of James 1:12, *"Blessed is the one who perseveres under trial because, having stood the test, that person will receive the crown of life that the Lord has promised to those who love him."*

Halfway through this process, my friend planned a going away party for me and invited three people as a surprise. The pastor that I broke down in front of two years prior showed up. It was nice seeing them again, and they prayed for a new chapter in my life. The pastor's wife gave me a crown necklace. It was another testimony that God used to help convince me I was doing the right thing. The next day I was meditating on my verse in a different version.

James 1:12, NIRV said, *"Blessed is the person who keeps on going when times are hard. **After they have come through tough times, this person will*** *receive a crown. The crown is life itself. The Lord has promised it to those who love him."*

The crown I had received from the pastor's wife the day before made me feel like I had received the crown from God. Now, the next chapter in my life was unknown.

Chapter Eleven

THE NEW BEGINNING

After twenty-eight years of being apart and living with the guilt of what had happened, Jon had forgiven me, and reconciliation took place. Neither one of us ever, in a million years, expected to see each other again.

The first time I saw him, the song, *"I'm Goin' Home,"* by Chris Tomlin played repeatedly in my head. He even pulled out our wedding pictures. How he still had them after being apart all those years and being married a second time without her seeing them was beyond my understanding. It was good to look at the pictures again and reunite with him after so much time.

He often said, "Who would have thunk (spelled correctly, that is how he said it) we would be together again."

We discussed renewing our marriage vows on the date we were originally married. We could enjoy our later life stress free, with no worries about having children. He had a daughter, and I had my son. God had given us a second chance to make things right. *Therefore, I tell you, her many sins have been forgiven—as her great love has shown." Luke 7:47*

This was the new chapter or beginning in my life. *'What does the future hold? Only the Lord knows, but I will do what I can to continue to be faithful to Him.'*

The opportunity came for me to get reconnected with his parents, sister and to meet his daughter. I was extremely nervous each time, but each encounter went very well. They accepted me back into their world. He even took the time to meet my family again at a scheduled family reunion.

The last time my family had been all together, thirty-two years before, was when Jon and I were married for the first time. It was such an exciting time to be together again. I could not believe coming back home allowed us to have this long-awaited reunion. From that point, my family planned to meet every year to stay connected more as a family and we started a group text as well. That way we could stay up to date on what was happening in our lives.

It was getting close to a new year, a time to enjoy the blessings of God! Christmas break was around the corner and Benjamin was flying out to spend time with me and to finally meet Jon and his dog. The encounter went better than expected. Even his dog was excited to meet Benjamin. The dog had never gotten up on the couch before but jumped on Benjamin's lap showing his acceptance. Christmas went well with his family, but what happened next was unexpected, and I needed time to completely trust in the Lord.

One week after Christmas, Jon was not feeling well. He went to get a CT scan (*Computerized Tomography x-ray images taken from different angles around the body*) that revealed he had a mass near his stomach. He received a doctor's referral that dealt with the digestive system. He started to lose his appetite to eat and the desire to workout. The doctor did an ultrasound scope to look more closely at the mass. The mass was in an area too difficult to reach without going through his pancreas and he referred him to another hospital which was more experienced with that type of biopsy of the mass. The hospital was able to get a sample and found out that he had cancer.

The PET scan (*Positron Emission Tomography that helps reveal functions of tissues and organs*) showed how far the cancer had traveled. The echo cardiogram made sure his heart was strong enough to endure chemo, and the doctor's prognosis report was diffuse large B cell lymphoma a.k.a. Non-Hodgkin's Lymphoma. Jon had to do a total of six chemo treatments: one every three weeks for four months. He was told the success rate was 60% for the treatment to work. Hearing about all the information and side effects was overwhelming. They wanted to do the first chemo treatment on the same day he had the other three appointments. His anxiety at that point was extremely high. He decided not to stay and scheduled the chemo treatment for another day. He also wanted time to absorb all the information he had just received.

The first chemo session went well but took eight hours to complete. The other chemo treatments took about four to five hours.

The days after the treatments varied in how he felt. He did not have many side effects, which was a blessing. It was simply hard to eat sometimes without his stomach feeling uncomfortable. He started to lose his hair with the treatments, but still looked handsome as ever.

He did receive sores on his lip but was able to heal quickly with ointment. Bills started coming in which caused more anxiety about how they were all going to be paid. God was faithful and each bill was paid on time.

The next scheduled PET scan was on the day we were going to renew our vows. The cancer had already caused a delay in us completing our marriage vows, but we had to postpone yet again. The result of the PET scan was that the cancer was gone! We were so excited that we could finally plan for our future together as husband and wife.

Months went by, and I waited patiently for the day when he was going to pop the question. In the meantime, we enjoyed our time together fishing. I caught my first fish, and everyone knew it.

I screamed so loud with excitement the ground crew came running over to see and took a picture of me holding my first fish ever. The third fish I caught later in the summer put a desire back in Jon's heart to buy a bass boat.

Chapter Twelve

WHY SO SOON

It was a normal celebration of my birthday at Jon's parents' house. Gifts were presented and opened, but Jon had a surprise gift. He got down on his knee right in front of his family and asked me to remarry him. The answer was an excited, "Yes!" The beginning of the marriage preparation began. We were not sure when to have the special day.

One morning, the date October 19 came to my mind, and I texted my sister to see if she was available on that day. Lo and behold, she had that weekend off from work. The result would be an outdoor wedding in our backyard on that day.

In the meantime, Jon decided he wanted to get a bass boat. The first boat he chose ended up being a fake ad on the internet. Thank God the bank caught it, or he would have lost the money he was investing in that boat. The boat he chose next was at the dealer in Alabama: everything he ever wanted in a bass boat and more. As he prepared to pick up the boat halfway, I was busy fixing up the basement and rearranging the house as a surprise for him. I cleaned out the garage to fit in the gigantic new boat that would take up half of it. He was a little startled when he saw the changes in the basement at first, but then was appreciative that I had made the changes.

I headed on a two-week road trip with my sister for a family reunion in Arizona. We made a stop in Texas to see one of my friends. While there, I asked my friend if we could do shopping in her closet.

My friend pulled out a wedding dress and a bridesmaid dress to wear at the wedding in October that fit perfectly on both of us. God was so good to supply everything for the wedding from the dresses, flowers, photographer, cake, and even a discount on decorations for the beautiful sunny day.

The day finally arrived! I prepared myself to be the most beautiful bride possible by getting my nails, hair, and makeup done by a professional. I wanted to look special for Jon. It took longer than expected to get ready and Jon was starting to get concerned about why it was taking us so long and when I would be back from the salon.

One thing I remember the makeup artist did was put smudge-free lipstick on me.

During the ceremony, Jon said something funny when he was repeating his vows, and it made him turn to his family and chuckle. Another funny thing happened when the pastor said, "You may kiss the bride." My so-called smudge-free lipstick did not just stay on me, but Jon was wearing it too! So much for smudge-free. I tried wiping it off before we turned to walk back down the aisle to no avail. Thank God it came off before taking pictures, another part of the day I was grateful for. It had only misted in the morning and then it rained *after* the pictures.

We were finally spouses again. Joy and love were in the air. Our future of hopes and dreams was fulfilled.

What happened next took the wind out of our sail.

Three days after our blissful wedding day, Jon had his six months cancer follow-up to make sure he was doing okay and still in remission. He shared with the doctor how he was having the urgency to use the bathroom often with no results and coughing a little more.

The doctor was concerned and scheduled for him to have a CT scan and the result was that the cancer had come back in his bladder.

Because the bladder wall increased in size it caused the urine to back up into the kidneys. He was admitted to the hospital that night and was beginning to feel his anxiety increasing again. The decision was for him to have tubes connected to his kidneys to drain the excess fluid. I drove back and forth for a week, an hour each way, until he was released from the hospital. They also had a chemo treatment that week. The next chemo would not take place for another three weeks.

One of Jon's favorite places to visit was the Marina. So, I took a picture of it on one of my trips back and forth to the hospital. I had forgotten to show it to him at the hospital and texted him the picture that night.

His response was: "Thx for putting a smile on my face. I had forgotten all about the marina. I LOVE YOU!"

He was so focused on what was happening to him that he could not think about anything else. He did not expect cancer to happen right after getting married. Our future hopes and plans felt crushed.

He would always say, "You never signed up for this!"

My response was, "No, but we will get through this together."

The day he had chemo was a grueling day. He did not start receiving the chemo until later in the afternoon. It made him a little irritable. I said something to the nurse about what was happening to his kidney draining, but do not remember what I said. Jon responded to me sternly, "Shut up!"

I was hurt by his tone of voice. I did not stay for his complete chemo treatment because it was getting late, and I needed to get back home for the dog. As I was driving home, I just cried. I felt bad for leaving him there by himself for the treatment. When I got home, I texted him saying I was sorry and to please forgive me for leaving early.

The day came for us to go home and adjust to the tubes coming out of his back. He was doing a little better at first. The coughing had stopped, and he was able to use the restroom again.

About two weeks later, he got a UTI (*Urinary Tract Infection that can affect the kidney, ureters, bladder, and urethra*).

We went to urgent care and had an antibiotic prescribed for the UTI. The first prescription was the wrong kind. He had to switch to another antibiotic that would have taken him into the next chemo treatment.

We went to the hospital on Friday to prepare for the next chemo. They drew labs and the doctor spoke to us to schedule another chemo session. It was scheduled for Monday instead. We were shocked by yet another trip to the hospital.

This began a sequence of events over the next three weeks that were both completely shocking to me and some of the hardest I've walked through. Through all of it, I kept holding on to the hope of life with Jon.

On the way to the new appointment, the car broke down and we had to wait two hours for the tow truck to arrive. In the meantime, Jon had to go to the bathroom in the bushes because around us was nothing but open fields.

On the second trip to use the restroom, I saw him fall, but he was okay. He happened to check his coat for his phone when he got back in the car, and he realized that it dropped out of his pocket when he fell. Since I saw where he fell, I got out of the car to find the phone. At the same time, the towing company showed up. I spotted the phone, thank God!

We had to reschedule the chemo treatment for the coming Wednesday. Because of the delay in having the chemo treatments, he was having problems with using the restroom again. Constipation started.

Wednesday

As we drove back to the hospital, it was hard for him to sit an hour drive. Even though we made a couple stops, his right leg started hurting. During the chemo treatment, the doctor came into the room, and Jon shared about how he was feeling. He also mentioned the constipation issue. The doctor just prescribed water pills, laxative, bladder stimulating pills, and pain pills then sent him home after the chemo was over.

After getting home, I noticed that he just did not seem the same. His eyes would become wide-looking, scary. I was also worried about the pain pills given to him because they can be very addictive.

Friday

His kidney tube on the right side was not working right. I called the doctor's office concerned about it. The doctor called back and said to come to the hospital immediately and they would look at the tube. They ended up changing it out.

On the way home, Jon mentioned going on a boating trip for our honeymoon down south near Kentucky in the coming spring. It was something to look forward to doing. I remained hopeful.

After getting home from the appointment, he no longer let me look at the bandages. I did notice that the tube they changed out was dark red and was not right.

Monday

He was still struggling with constipation, so he went to his primary doctor who had him go to a specialty.

Wednesday

He went to see the specialist, and they only gave him cream to put on his bottom end.

After coming home from the specialist, he asked me to schedule an appointment with the primary again about his burning feeling when urinating. So, I called, and they would not be available until Monday, and said to call the chemo doctor that he had been working with.

The chemo nurse called us back and said to go to the ER (*Emergency Room*) locally, because of the holiday coming up. He did not want to go.

Thursday

Finally, on Thanksgiving Night, he agreed to go to the ER the next morning.

Friday

We went to the local hospital ER at 6:00 am. They ran tests and took blood work. The doctor, at that time, said the cancer had spread to his colon. He said for me to get an ambulance ride to the other hospital that had been working with his cancer. I teared up a little at that moment. I also saw the nurse tried to hide her tears as well. I still did not understand the seriousness of his condition, though.

The ambulance took him to the new location. I had to go home and make sure Benjamin was okay and get things that Jon would need in the hospital. After arriving in the ER, I had to watch them put a catheter in that hurt terribly. He kept telling them, "Stop!" but they continued inserting it.

As they were getting ready to transport him to an available room, I noticed a sheet of paper that had the report from the local ER. I took a picture of it to look at later. I decided to stay to wait for the diagnosis before leaving to go home. They said they would be putting new tubes in his back the next day sometime. Thinking he was going to be okay, I left to go home.

Once home, I looked over the diagnosis from the local ER. It said UTI, Sepsis. So, I looked up what sepsis was. It said it was a bacterial poison in the blood that was extremely dangerous and fatal.

Saturday

I got up the next morning planning to just stay at the hospital. I had Jon's sister take Benjamin to the airport to head back home. I arrived back at the hospital in time for the surgery. Jon did not have a good night's sleep, and his IV (*intravenous or in the vein*) machine was beeping after I arrived. So, I got the nurse because it was saying low battery. I did not think anything more about the IV issue.

They told me the surgery went well. The nurse brought in a cot for me to sleep on at night.

Jon was still struggling with pain, so they gave him pain medicine in his IV and antibiotics. That night his right leg was still in pain and his bottom end hurt sitting too long. The nurses tried a heating pad and a patch on his leg but neither worked. His legs started to swell. The only thing that relieved the pain was sitting on the toilet. All night long, I struggled with keeping him comfortable.

Every 10 minutes I would help him move from the bed to the bathroom and back to avoid catching the IV machine and catheter. At that time, it hit me, '*No wonder his battery was low on the IV machine when I came in this morning.*' He was taking himself to the bathroom the night before and was not able to plug it back in.

At one point, I finally got him comfortable on the cot and the nurse came in to take vitals. Well, his arm was close to the wall, and she could not reach it to get a blood test from the PICC (*Peripherally Inserted Central Catheter this helps to retrieve blood or insert chemo medication into the body easier*) in his left arm. So, he had to sit up, but she could not get any blood to come out. She flushed it four times and nothing. I then had to hold him standing up while he was in pain as she continued to try and draw blood from his PICC. We were both exhausted from a long night of moving and pain.

Sunday

Dehydration had set in, and he had low sodium, so they started giving him more liquids in his IV. He was beginning to swell even more. The doctors did more tests on him.

I had another long night of taking care of my husband and he was every 20 minutes sitting on the toilet to relieve the pain. I had to lift his legs to get him back into the bed because he could not lift them anymore by himself. He got in the habit of saying, "One, two, and three, up." Doctors were not talking to us about any test results. I asked the female doctor if he had sepsis, and her response was no.

Monday

They did more tests on him, and they removed the catheter that morning. Another long night followed where the 20 minutes moved to an hour on the toilet.

The nurse had to place the catheter back in because of fluid building back up in his bladder, and they also did an ultrasound on his heart. They found a mass there, either an infection or tumor. Because he was having this procedure done on his heart, they said he was not allowed to drink water.

So, I had to do my best to keep him from drinking and at one point, he sipped water from the bathroom sink.

Still, at that point, we were not expecting to stay in the hospital. Eventually we thought we would be able to go home.

Tuesday

We learned it would be too hard to get a biopsy for the area with the mass without causing any damage. The chemo doctor finally came in and talked to us about not being able to do anymore chemo treatments because his kidneys were at 20%. He did mention something about it leading to death.

I was concerned about how soon I should let his family know when to see him. The doctor said, "It would be a good idea to contact them now." I contacted the family to visit on Jon's birthday, which was the coming Friday.

Wednesday

The nurse came in and said, "Here are your morning medications," and named six different medications.

I was a little disturbed by that point and responded, "Do not give me the name of the drug because that does not make any sense to me. What are all the medications for?"

The fluid they were giving him was really making him swell up. I decided it would be best if the family was there earlier than Friday. His family was planning to show up at noon that day. The doctor was willing to talk to them. They visited for a little bit and then went home.

By this time, I was starting to get overly tired and emotional. I shared my state with the nurse, asking, "Why all the tests? For what?" and I showed her the diagnosis from the ER locally.

She said, "They are going to do another test where he will have to drink a gallon of water and then hold it for an hour."

I said, "*What*?! He cannot do that."

I was livid and asked to talk with the on-duty Chaplin. I poured out my heart to him about what was happening with all the tests and all the drugs they were putting in him and how they were pushing the chemo treatments.

He said he would talk with the morning Chaplin, who would talk with the team of doctors.

I got back to the room, and they were getting ready to gurney him for the ultrasound test.

I said, "*Stop*! I want to talk with the nurse."

The nurse said, "He will not have to drink the liquid like she said earlier."

That night Jon said in front of the nurse and me, "Done. I want to pass away and leave this earth."

Thursday

The first nurse I talked about sepsis with, who denied it, mentioned the word urosepsis (*sepsis caused by infections of the urinary tract*), probably because I showed the night nurse the ER report. I was still in shock that she mentioned the word and did not say anything more.

The kidney doctor talked with me as well. He shared that there were a couple of options: either hospice or palliative. I was at the point of having to decide. If I did hospice at home, I would be doing more work and I was already exhausted. I decided to have him go to a palliative upstairs in CCU (*Critical Care Unit used for those who have serious or life threating illnesses*).

I was hoping that this would be a better fit! When I got in the room at the CCU location, a counselor was in the room and mentioned that Jon may only have 1 to 4 days left to live. His breathing was slowing down.

One good thing out of all this so far, was that the music therapist came in and played his favorite song and made him smile, swaying his arms to the music, and he sang the song.

I called his sister to come and stay with me that night for moral support. It was getting to be too much. Drugged up, he did not know who I was.

His sister and daughter came. I still helped Jon during the night. He kept needing water and new sleeping positions. I tested the waters in the CCU to see how helpful the nurse would be. I would go get the nurse, not wanting to wake up his sister and daughter by buzzing the button, to rotate him.

Friday

The next morning, the head nurse came in and said, "We only rotate a patient every hour."

It was Jon's birthday. I was getting upset with the help in the hospital. I thought, *'Fine, I will do it myself then.'* His sister contacted the pastor, and he came and prayed with Jon to receive Jesus in his heart. It was a touching moment, especially for me, because I wanted him to have Jesus in his heart so badly. The day had now become both his physical and spiritual birth. It was a light in that dark time.

"…. If you declare with your mouth, "Jesus is Lord," and believe in your heart that God raised him from the dead, you will be saved." Romans 10:9

The family left, and I was alone with Jon again. That night I did ask for help to take him to the bathroom. Another joke! Three nurses came in to take him. He was so drugged up, they put him in a wheelchair that was too big to fit in the bathroom, so they brought in a Porta Potty to sit on. He wanted the toilet, and they kept saying it was.

He was getting frustrated with them; plus, who can go to the bathroom with people watching? They got him back in bed and left the room. I then helped him to the bathroom by myself.

When he was ready to go back to bed, the nurse just happened to come in and helped get him to bed. Two more times I took him by myself to the bathroom. Not wanting to disturb the nurses, I had to lift him in bed with the help of God.

I cried out repeatedly to God, "God give me strength and help me to position him in the bed right." I repositioned him three times every hour that night by myself with God's help.

Saturday

Jon was ready to get out of the hospital and go home. The family decided it would be best to have a hospice house. They allowed me to get sleep while they worked out the details. The plan was to go the next day because that was when it would be available.

I repeatedly said to Jon, "Just one more night and we will be out of here."

That night they finally gave him extra strong anxiety medicine that allowed him to sleep. He was hot and always had a fan on him. He kept trying to take his gown off, so I took it off him to make him more comfortable but covered him up with the sheet.

At one point, when the nurse came in, he had taken his covers off and was naked. She did not have the audacity to at least cover up his privates. She just took looks as she did his vitals. It disturbed me that she did not cover him up but just stared at him.

Thank God it was the first night of sleep in nine days, but only a 2-hour and 4-hour slot. Why they did not give him anxiety medicine before I don't know. He was a very anxious person to see a doctor and considering everything he had been through, he needed it.

Sunday

In the morning, they prepared for the departure to go to the hospice house. The ambulance came to take him. As they were taking him to the vehicle, I saw tears in his eyes, and I wiped them away. It made me cry, too.

When we got to the hospice house, they did an assessment of his condition. Do you know what? The first thing they worked on was his bottom end, which the hospital never even addressed.

The family arrived again. I decided to take a break and go home to our dog and pack some more things so I could stay with Jon.

When I finally got back to the hospice house around 9:00 pm, his parents seemed disturbed I had taken so long to come back.

In the middle of the night, I noticed that his breathing was becoming more of a gargling sound. I asked the nurse about it.

She said, "He cannot swallow anymore."

As they came in to rotate him, I asked to lie next to him, and they accommodated me.

During the early morning, I whispered to him, "I love you. I did the best I could to take care of you. I am so sorry you had to go through all of this."

Not seconds had gone by when he took his last three breaths. I just cried and cried; for how long I do not know.

Poem from his Funeral Memorial Card:

> *God looked around the garden and found an empty space.*
> *He looked down upon the Earth and saw your tired face.*
> *He put his arms around you and lifted you to rest.*
> *God's garden must be beautiful for He only takes the best.*
> *He knew that you were weary, and He knew you were in pain.*
> *He knew that you would never be well on Earth again.*
> *He saw the roads were getting rough and hills were hard to climb.*
> *So, He closed your weary eyelids and whispered, "Peace be thine."*

I finally got up the strength and courage to tell the nurse he just passed away. The nurse came in and assessed him. He had.

I was shaking so much that I had a tough time calling anyone, so the nurse called family and friends to tell them.

The love of my life was gone, just seven weeks after our joyous reuniting in marriage. I was deeply saddened, but I knew that God had brought me back into his life to help him through this process.

I am grateful and glad to know that he is now in heaven with God. He is in a better place with no more pain, sorrow, or tears.

I just needed to get through the pain, sorrow, and tears here on earth until I see him again. What a joyful day that will be!

I remembered the song when I saw Jon for the first time again.

I'm Goin' Home
by Chris Tomlin

This world is not what it was meant to be.
All this pain, all this suffering
There's a better place waiting for me in Heaven.
Every tear will be wiped away.
Every sorrow and sin erased.
We'll dance on seas of amazing grace in Heaven.
I'm goin' home.

Where the streets are golden
Every chain is broken.
Oh, I wanna go Home.
Where every fear is gone
I'm in your open arms.
Where I belong
Lay down my burdens, I lay down my past.
I run to Jesus, no turning back.

Now I knew why the song kept playing repeatedly in my mind when we first met after all those years apart. God was letting me know back then that Jon would be going to be with Him soon. God was already preparing my heart for the day when Jon would be with the Lord forever. He was goin' home.

Some more healing needed to take place in my life to find a new normal.

Chapter Thirteen

THE PROCESS

It was time to move to the next phase of my life. It was hard without Jon with me. I was saddened by the loneliness of the home without my husband. I cried every day trying to heal from the pain of losing him.

I committed myself to doing the *Experiencing God* study with a friend. As I read it again for the 17th time, I felt still touched by how God speaks to me in ways I need. Each time I have gone through the study, I have been in a new stage of my life, so different words speak to me.

For example, when God called me to leave everything behind and move closer to Jon, the whole purpose was so that I could be there to help draw Jon closer to God and help him through the illness of cancer. I had no idea this was going to happen. If I would have known all the details before moving forward in where God was leading me, would I have gone through it? I don't know. I think I would because of my love for Jon. We were true soulmates separated temporarily to grow into more mature individuals.

The timing was right, and every detail God worked out. We were meant to be together again at that time in his life. Over the years we tried connecting, but the timing was always off. A friend of his told me that he never stopped loving me and regretted letting me go. One of his favorite songs on his playlist was by Cher, "If I could turn back time." I bet every time he listened to that song, he thought of me. And it was second on his favorite list, so I know he listened to it often. Here are the words in the song:

If I could turn back time If I could find a way
I'd take back those words that hurt you and you'd stay.
I don't know why I did the things I did.
I don't know why I said the things I said.
Loves like a knife it can cut deep inside
Words are like weapons, they wound sometimes.
I didn't really mean to hurt you.
I didn't want to see you go.
I know I made you cry.
My world was shattered, I was torn apart.
Like someone took a knife and drove it deep in my heart
You walked out that door I swore that I didn't care.
But I lost everything darling then and there.
Too strong to tell you I was sorry
Too proud to tell you I was wrong.

Today as I write this, I am still in tears. I do visit the grave site every day sharing my life and how I am feeling. I cried out "WHY, WHY, WHY! I do not understand, God, why You give and take away!"

Every day someone tells me what a great guy he was and that they are sorry for my loss. I just do not know how to respond anymore but thank you and try not to cry. I sensed that through the *Experiencing God* study, Jon sent me a note. Saved and excited. It said:

Dear Julie,

Merry Christmas! It is the first Christmas with Jesus in my heart. I knew God sent you to me, and I could deny him no longer. He saved me! Happy New Year! (Blackaby & King, 2005, p. 39)

Love,
Jon

I decided to attend a grief group to help in my healing process at the hospice house. It was an 8-week group for spousal loss. The group was okay. I was the youngest one in the group and felt a little out of place. I did more listening than speaking.

I cried every day, wondering if the pain would ever end. The "what if's" really bothered me. What if I prayed more, what if I spoke up earlier, and what if I did more to help him live longer?

I have beaten myself up over things I cannot change. I kept wondering what our life together could have been like now that we were married again.

I attended a movie at a church called "Faith Song." I was not expecting the ending to be as it was. There was a couple in the movie that lost their child prematurely at the same time her sister was pregnant. Sixteen years later the sister passed away in a car accident and their child went to this couple for care. Losing their child brought back sad memories of me never being able to have one for sixteen years.

At the end of the movie, the couple sat by their child's grave. It had the date: May 1998. Probably because I was crying so hard, it looked like 1986 to me. It hit my heart. That was the month, May, and the year, 1986, that Jon and I got married for the first time. I left the church in tears and went to Jon's grave site to tell him what I had just seen. I was terribly upset, so that when I got back into the car I cried out to God and said, "I am so mad right now and hurt that You did not allow me to bear Jon a child when we were first married. Why? I do not understand." Days later it hit me, I had never really grieved my barrenness. This gave me closure for Jon's death and the inability to have children with him. God wanted me healed from both tragedies in my life.

While I was doing my *Experiencing God* study again, I was at the chapter that talked about how God speaks by the Holy Spirit through the Bible. Here was my experience on the word study for Grief.

John 16:22 *"...Now is your time of grief, but I will see you again and you will rejoice, and no one will take away your joy."*

"Lord, was it my husband telling me that I would see him again? I will rejoice because I know he has been with You all this time. I can rejoice and be glad."

1 Thessalonians 5:14 *"I believe that Jesus died and rose again and so I believe that God will bring with Jesus those who have fallen asleep in Him."*

"Lord, thank You that when Jesus returns, He will bring my husband with Him as one of His saints. I am thankful for his salvation."

Revelations 21:4 *"God will wipe every tear from my eyes. There will be no more death or mourning or crying or pain..."*

"Thank You, Lord, for comforting me by holding all my tears in Your hands. There will be a time of no mores.... Thank You, God, for Your comfort and love."

Matthew 14:13-14 footnotes on Jesus' example of how He grieved: *Jesus did not dwell on His grief but returned to the ministry He came to do.*

"Lord, help me to not dwell on Jon's death anymore, but move on to the ministry You have for me."

After that time with God, I finally felt at peace and content.

I visited Jon's grave and told him that I would not be visiting him daily anymore, but only on special occasions.

During church service this verse was shared: Revelations 2:10, and footnotes that spoke to my heart.

"Do not be afraid of what you are about to suffer. I tell you, the devil will.... evaluate you, and you will suffer... for ten days... Be faithful, even to the point of death, and I will give you a crown of life."

The footnote said, "Believers need not fear death, because it will only result in their receiving the crown of life. Satan may harm the earthly bodies, but he can do them no spiritual harm. Pain is part of life, but it is never easy to suffer, no matter what the cause. If you are experiencing challenging times, do not let them turn you away from God. Instead let them draw you toward greater faithfulness to Him. Trust God, and remember your heavenly reward, eternal life."

This touched my heart because my husband suffered in the hospital for ten days, and received the crown of life, eternal life with Christ Jesus. He stayed faithful to the end. Whenever I was going through a tough time, my husband would always tell me, "Keep the faith!" It always kept me going knowing that God has everything under His control and in His timing.

Chapter Fourteen

TOUGH DECISIONS

My life took another turn. I had to take care of Jon's Estate. In the state of Illinois, if there is not a Will when a spouse dies, everything is divided 50/50 between the surviving spouse and the children through probate.

I truly recommend that you make a Will or Trust for your family. It is not a painless process in dealing with an Estate. There are huge decisions to make, and you pray that you make the right ones along the way.

The first thing was to get the paperwork I could find on Jon's assets and liabilities together. Once I got this information in order, I went to the courthouse to get the house placed in my name because Jon had wanted me to have it whenever he passed away. The only thing was my name was not on the deed of the house. That was when I found out that I would have to go through probate to get it managed correctly.

I was referred to an attorney who might be able to help. When I went in to see him, I was still an emotional wreck. This all took place before my healing from Jon. The attorney was not able to help with probate situations but referred me to another attorney who managed those kinds of cases. So, I contacted this other attorney and scheduled a time to meet with her after coming back from my trip to see my son march for band in the Rose Parade in California.

When I got back from my trip, I found out that Jon's daughter also now had an attorney. This made the process longer and more difficult. I was responsible to oversee the administration of Jon's Estate.

The life insurance policy had her as the beneficiary, so she was able to receive that with no questions asked. His pension's death benefit also went to her because she was the beneficiary. Since he had no spouse at the time of his retirement, it said that he was still divorced on the policy. Because of that and the fact that I was newly married to him less than a year before his death, he lost all his pension.

The house had no mortgage, but for me to be able to get the house, I would have to buy his daughter out. I was working part-time with no way of getting a loan to pay for the house.

Plus, I thought it was crazy to put a loan on a house with no mortgage. I suggested that I could pay her in payments until my portion of the house was paid, but that only ended with a letter from her attorney that she was not a lending service and that she eventually wanted me to pay rent to live in the house. The same one that I was living in with Jon before he passed away! I was shocked when I got that letter. It was about four months after his passing. Was she expecting me to pay for the last few months? I did not have the funds to do such a thing and I was also wondering what the monthly rent was going to be. I was panicking!

I talked with my attorney, and she said I would not have to do that, which was a relief. I still had a nervous breakdown over it. I remember calling my sister crying hysterically, and she just kept saying, "Breathe, take a deep breath," to calm me down. After a while, I was calm and pulled myself back together to keep moving forward in the process.

In the meantime, going through all of it, I had the responsibility of taking care of my mom, Sally. She had developed dementia and could not be by herself. I was not able to help right away because of my work situation. So, she temporarily stayed at the nursing home with her husband until I was able to get her.

The day my sister and I went to take my mother out of the nursing home was the same day Covid lock down took place. We discharged her earlier in the morning in order to take care of paperwork and put my name on her things, since I became her power of attorney. When we went back to the nursing home, we could not get in because of the lock down. If we had showed up minutes later, she would have stayed there. She was able to come live with me until I was able to figure out what was going to happen to me and my situation.

My sister and I moved my mother up from Arkansas to live with me. This was a hard transition for Sally because she was leaving her spouse, who was in the nursing home, and the place she lived to go to the unknown. I then agreed that once the probate was over, we would move back down to Arkansas. We kept her apartment and only moved items that would fit in my house.

After living in my/Jon's house for a month, Sally decided she would not mind moving to Illinois permanently. Well, this was during the time of census, so I filled out the paperwork and did not know where to put us living. I chose Illinois over Arkansas. Since we were in Illinois and all Sally's things were in Arkansas, we planned to drive the 9-hour drive there the next day to get her things and let go of the apartment there.

Our journey was interesting. Sally drove her van, and I drove Jon's truck to Arkansas. When we arrived, the only way into her apartment was the remote control to the garage. Well guess what? We could not find the remote anywhere. I thought, '*Great we left it back in Illinois.*'

We walked to the back of Sally's apartment and the window to her husband's bedroom opened. Even though I had long legs, I had to reach high to get in. I climbed in feet first and did the limbo to find the floor on the other side. Once I got into the house, I unlocked the back door for Sally.

Next, she wanted to take her outdoor swing with her to Illinois. It could come apart. I asked the person next door if they had any tools we could borrow. They said, "Yes!" and came over to help. While doing that, one of the poles fell on my back. I thought, '*What else can go wrong?*'

A second later, the cat disappeared. Sally started to freak out. I told her, "Go into the house and relax. I will go and look for your cat." Her cat was in the shed next to the house. The cat would not come to me, and I could not reach her because of the small entry to the shed. I asked the neighbor that was helping us with taking apart the swing to get Sally so she could get the cat out of the shed. I continued waiting for what seemed like hours, but it was only minutes. The neighbor walked back to where I was but had forgotten to tell Sally to come. So, I had to wait even longer. Sally came but her cat did not want to come out. I went in to get food to see if that would help and the cat finally came out.

While getting the rest of the things in the van and on the truck, I noticed the garage door opener behind the driver's seat of the van. I just laughed that I had to go through all the struggle to get into the house.

The next day we headed back to Illinois early in the morning. I was a little nervous about it because Sally was driving so much in a brief period. She followed me home swerving. Yikes! We made it back safely. Since we got back late, we decided to unload the vehicles the next day.

Because Sally wanted the bigger bedroom to stay in, I decided it would be best for me to move the current bed to the basement since it was waterproof. Sally and I moved the queen size mattress down the stairs. I said, "We don't need no man, we can do it ourselves." But guess what? What we found at the end of the stairs of the basement was the mattress did not fit the opening. Thank God mattresses can bend a little. We were able to get the mattress on the floor in the basement, finally. "But what are we going to do with the box spring?" '*We are never going to get it in the basement,*' I thought.

As soon as we got upstairs, one of Jon's guy friends stopped by to make sure I was doing okay after his death. He was so kind in helping us unload the rest of the items in the vehicles. He knew someone that sold twin box springs that I could buy so that the mattress would not be on the floor. That was nice of him.

Sally settled in the house, and I had to finish focusing on the probate process of getting rid of the truck, boat, and items in the house and deciding if they would be sold in a garage sale, given away, or thrown away.

I gave Jon's daughter the opportunity to come through the house and take anything that she wanted. I asked my attorney if everything else was mine to deal with and she said, "Yes!"

I started going through his things to get them ready for a garage sale. I was able to sell things, but his daughter expected me to put the money into the estate. I said, "No, you took what you wanted and the rest I have to deal with as I so choose." She was not happy about that at all. It started friction between us from that point on. She felt I did not deserve anything since I was only married to Jon for a month and half. Yet I dealt with everything.

I had to return the truck to the car dealership because it was going to auction if no more payments were paid. We were able to have them just take over the payments, which was a deal for them because it was low mileage and only a couple of years old. I tried selling it but with Covid going on, people did not want to buy sizable items because they had lost their jobs or were unable to work.

We also had the boat Jon had bought three months before his passing to get rid of. There was a large debt on it, and we could not afford to make the payments. I was able to find a boat dealer that would collaborate with me on trying to sell it.

Because of the struggle I was going through, I shared it with my sister who talked with one of her attorney friends. I was able to at least receive a widow's benefit for my spouse passing away. This was an immense help in all the things that were about to happen. I did not receive the funds right away, but at least I knew I had something to help take care of Sally and myself.

About two months after Sally settled in the home, we had to put the house up for sale. What a stressful time! I had to find a new place to live. *'Do I stay in Illinois, or do we move back down to Arkansas?'* We decided to move to be closer to her husband in the nursing home.

Well, this was a hard transition because I had let go of her apartment. Now where would we live? We were living on Sally's Social Security because I was not able to work; she could not be home alone for an extended period. I had to let go of the full-time job I had just received through the school district. When finding an apartment, they wanted us to fill out an application and pay a fee to go with it.

I was finally able to find a realtor that was willing to help us if we paid three months upfront. It was not a delightful place but what were we going to do? We could always keep looking for another place once we got there.

I rented a 10ft U-Haul truck to move the items that we still had left in the house. U-Haul was so kind to upgrade us to the next size at no added cost, a 15ft truck. We also had her van to pull behind the truck with a wheel tow. On moving day, God supplied helpers from church, a neighbor, and even my cousin. I said we would supply pizza for the moving day event and the Lord also provided. I happened to go to a neighbor's house to get a tool to take the T.V. down. While there, a person was delivering pizzas that they were trying to get rid of.

I said, "I know the perfect place. You will find a U-Haul truck around the corner. It will bless the helpers if you drop the pizza off there."

It was amazing to see His provision. We were loaded up and ready to head down to Arkansas. I was nervous about driving something so large. God again helped me do this; without Him I do not know how I would have done it.

Once I got there, we could not find the place to meet the realtor. Finally, we got to the apartment, and I thought, *'What have I done?'* It was not a delightful place. The screen door had torn from the door, and there were rat holes in the closets. We unloaded the U-Haul but did not unpack our boxes in the hope that we would not be there long. It was a Thursday.

On Friday, we spent the day looking at other locations to move into. The place where we were going to live still had the electricity and water in the last person's name, though we were not sure for how long. I kept trying to get them to switch it over into my mom's name, but I kept getting the run around.

So, I went back to the realtor to see if they could help. They gave us directions, "You will see a fire station and school. Behind the fire station you will see the place to take care of the water hookup."

Sally and I drove for about ten miles it seemed and never found it. I took mom back to the apartment while I figured out what to do. I sat in the grocery store parking lot just crying out to my sister because my cell phone did not work in the apartment without internet. I said, "What have I done? I messed everything up. I let go of her earlier apartment, and this place is a dive. I do not know if I can continue to do this."

At the same time, my friend from Texas just happened to call me. Again, this was a God encounter. She was willing to help get me set up in a hotel for the weekend.

Still, I could not do anything until Monday since nothing was open on the weekend. I could not deal with the electricity or water hookup. I thanked my friend and headed back to the apartment, only to find out that the water had been shut off.

Monday came and we were able to find another apartment to move to. We gradually made the transition to the new location. It was better, but it did have mold on the windows that made Sally, and I sick for a little bit before we got it cleaned up. We were able to get the money back for not staying for the three months. Thank you again, God, for provision. We were finally settled and comfortable in our new place.

After I moved to Arkansas, the stress of probate was not as bad. I was no longer living so close to everything. I sold the boat and the heartache of dealing with everything ended. I was glad it was over.

"Trust in the Lord with all your heart and lean not on your own understanding; in all your ways acknowledge Him, and He will make your paths straight." Proverbs 3:5-6

Chapter Fifteen

STARTING OVER

Sally and I continued living the new normal life. We visited her husband through the window of the nursing home because of Covid and the continued lockdown of the facility. We attended church service and took walks around the creek in the neighborhood. Since we did not have a laundry facility in our apartment, we went to the laundry mat.

One day while doing laundry, a man came in to do his laundry. We struck up a conversation and eventually became good friends. However, because I get cold sores on the mouth, a form of herpes, we never became more than just friends. The cold sores made it difficult for me to find a new partner. I even learned of a medicine that I could take to suppress the outbreak of cold sores, but still never knew when or if it would show its ugly head again.

After being back in Arkansas only a couple of months, Sally's spouse passed away from the Covid virus that was going around the nursing home. With the recent loss of Jon, I was able to help comfort Sally as best as I could. She seemed to handle it better than I thought she would. On her hard days of missing him and grieving more than other days, I would patiently listen as she shared what she was experiencing. Sometimes just sitting quietly holding her hand or hugging her made her feel loved, and it helped the healing process for her.

Five months later, at the exact same laundry mat, Sally found a new partner. They were getting along well. The only problem was my mother was jealous of him talking to me. This caused great tension between us to the point where I was ready to just give up and leave. She ended up moving in with him instead.

It caused me to live by myself. I did not want to be alone, so I started looking into dating apps online. I talked to one man who grabbed my attention. He was from another state but decided to visit me. He was a Christian man. He bought a one-way ticket and ended up staying with me, until I no longer felt comfortable. All he wanted from me was sex and when I cut him off, he treated me as if I was worthless! Every time I turned around, he would say that something else was wrong with me, but he was the best at everything he did. I could not take it anymore and sent him back home.

I continued looking for another man on the site, but nothing grabbed my heart for some time, until I saw a profile of someone that did not want to have sex until he was married. I really liked that because that was what I wanted too.

During that time, I had to decide on where I was going to live once the lease was up on my current apartment. I kept going back and forth thinking *'Do I stay in Arkansas, or do I go back to Illinois?'* I planned to move back to Illinois to live with my sister.

Before moving in with her, I went to visit this new man in his town, the one I had seen on the app. He provided me with a separate home to stay in to remove any form of temptation. I stayed there for a month. I helped him with home repairs and really considered staying there, but I was not attracted to him. I tried sticking it out. On the day I left for my Family Reunion, I was very emotional, which he was not prepared to deal with. He ended up breaking it off with me. I was relieved because I think I would have just settled and that would not have lasted long term. My sister could tell that I was not into him by the tone of my voice when I talked with her about him.

Once I was living with my sister, still wishing I had a man in my life, I got back on the online dating app. I talked to and thought I found another guy that had potential. But all he did was sweetly talk me into giving him money: a scam romance through the dating site. So yes, I was a victim of the fake guy on the other end of the phone. I stuck it out for seven months of heartache and stress. God kept warning me through people, but I wanted to believe that he was real. He kept saying he was real and that he would pay me back once he arrived in the states. He kept saying he was coming home, but every day it was time for him to come home, it was another excuse why he could not make it and would need more money.

God finally spoke to me in a dream that woke me up to the reality of what was happening. The dream was about this guy biting my neck and sucking my blood from me. Then I saw a bumble bee that was stuck in the dry blood and could not get unstuck.

My interpretation of this dream was that he was going to suck me dry financially and I would BE stuck in it and would not be able to get out of it. I was at the point of giving him access to a bank account in my name, where he would deposit money into the account, but the reality was he was just going to use my name and rack up the debt.

So, ladies, do not let any man sweet talk you into liking them. IT IS NOT REAL! I learned my lesson the hard way.

But I thank my God for not giving up on me and making a way out for me to not continue in the fake relationship.

I stopped online for a while, but then started the process again because was lonely. I met the next few guys face to face, but they were just out for sex. I dumped them quickly. I was not going to go in that direction again. I wanted to stay pure this time around. I became wiser in my choices and stopped a conversation as soon as a red flag showed up or if they had something that I knew I could not live with long term. The last guy I finally stopped talking to was going to be another money experience. He talked sweetly to me for a week on the phone and reminded me of the first guy that asked for money.

Thank God I learned my lesson from the first time.

I am praying for God to supply the right person for me. He can answer that prayer in His timing. I must be patient and wait! I gave up on online dating. I wasted time and money, but it helped me to grow in knowing what I genuinely want in a relationship and what I do not want. I encourage any ladies out there to be meticulous with who you are dating. Do not just settle for the next guy that may like you. Really wait for God and pray for Him to supply the right partner for you. He will. But first He wants to be the most intimate person in your life. God wants a love relationship with you. And through that relationship He will supply and give you the desires of your heart.

"But look for first the kingdom of God and His righteousness, all these things will be given to you as well. Therefore, do not worry about tomorrow, for tomorrow will worry about itself. Each day has enough trouble of its own." Matthew 6:33-34

Chapter Sixteen

THE RIGHT CHOICE

"I am still confident of this; I will see the goodness of the Lord in the land of the living. Wait for the Lord; be strong and take heart and wait on the Lord."
Psalm 27:13-14

May 2023, three and a half years after my husband passed away, and I chose to wait for the Lord to bring the right person into my life. I decided I was not going to rush the process. If it will be, it will be. I do not have to force it, convince it, manipulate it, or worry about it.

In the meantime, I continued to develop my relationship with the Lord.

It is an ongoing sanctification process.

Each time I go through the *Experiencing God* study, it is different.

This time my assignment is to take off the grave clothes: things in my past that I may still be holding on to.

I asked the Holy Spirit to reveal to me any area of my life that I need to let go of or need healing. The area that He showed me to work on was my sexuality. It is a weakness of mine and hard to resist. I came across a book called *How to Stay Pure Before Your Wedding Night* by Author Unknown. This is my prayer.

"Lord God, You know how I have struggled to have a man in my life and the desire for physical affection. I want to stay pure before You and honor You with my body, but I will need Your help to teach me how to say No! When the passion arises, help me to have self-control and live a godly upright life. Give me the strength to wait on the right man You have created for me. May our waiting for the wedding night be so special and truly blessed beyond measure because we stayed faithful to You and each other.

"Forgive me for all my past sexual relationships I had and remove all soulties. In the Mighty name of Jesus, make me into a purified virgin woman again. Thank you for Your healing power and Your grace and forgiveness. Make me whole again! Keep me shielded from worldly passion. God reveal to me what part of my heart needs purification. It has been misled before, and I do not want my heart to be misled anymore. Open my eyes to any red flag quickly, see clearly and move on. Lord, I commit with Your help to do the following:

"I will not discuss marriage to him until he romantically and lovingly makes a commitment to ask me to marry him.

"I will not discuss sex, physical contact, or my desires with him.

"I will communicate a desire to live a lifestyle of purity."

I sensed God saying to me: Simply join your life to MINE! Abstinence!!! Premarital sex prohibited. Avoid all types of intimate contact. Wait until you have found the right person! Live as one who has died to every form of sexual sin and impurity. Take drastic measures to stay pure.

As I was reading the book, *How to Stay Pure Before Your Wedding Night,* the topic of a lizard came up. It brought me back to that dream I had a long time ago.

I prayed: "Lord God, I am helpless here. I need that little lizard of lust, guy craziness, to leave me now in the name of Jesus. Destroy that lizard on my shoulder Lord. Hurl it to the ground, step on it and kill it. Even though I have sinned in this area of my life, I ask for Your forgiveness and will no longer hide from You Lord but run to You for my fulfillment. Thank You, Jesus for removing this from my life and killing it forever. Help me keep my eyes on You. "

June 2023, I prayed, "Abba Father, I thank You and praise You for bringing me back from my darkness that was overtaking me. Thank you for opening my eyes to see that I went down the wrong path. Heal me from my herpes. You are so loving, and You even accept me back and desire to heal me. I am thankful.

"Lord, it brings me to tears knowing that You absolutely love me even though I have made mistakes in my life. I completely surrender my WHOLE life to You now to use however You see me fitting into Your plans and purpose. As I prepare for what lies ahead, I trust in You to supply all that I will need. Go before me and lead me as we do this journey together. I can only do it with YOU by my side. I surrender now to all that You have for me to do. I am Your servant, use me for Your glory. In Jesus name, amen."

Dare to believe!

I took a step of faith and threw away my herpes medication believing that I am healed from it! I have not had an outbreak ever since. Praise the Lord.

November 2023 came, and I did the *Experiencing God* Study again.

I sensed God saying to me:

God: What I could not do in my own strength, NOW I will do in His Strength. (Blackaby, 1990, p. 49)

Me: I must trust God to help me stay pure as I move forward in my convictions to not have sex before marriage.

God: Gen 22 footnote: God tested Abraham, not trip him, and watch him fall, but to deepen his capacity to obey God and thus develop his character.

When I am tested, I will see how God is stretching me to develop my character. Obeying God is often a struggle because it means giving up something we truly want or desire.

I did a word study on "testing", and this was my conversation with God.

God: Gen 22:7-8 footnote: The purpose of testing is to strengthen my character and deepen my commitment to God and His perfect timing.

Me: Lord God, I want to be stronger in my character and walk with a deeper commitment to You. I know Your timing is always best. Continue to grow my heart to be ready for this encounter. I need to allow You to strengthen my character and deepen my walk with You. Because without You, I will fail the test. Keep me strong Lord.

God: Luke 4:1 footnote: When facing this trail, be careful to follow faithfully whatever the Holy Spirit leads me to do. Be always on my guard.

Me: Lord God I can do this only with Your help. So, I ask that You prepare my heart and to strengthen me through this test. Help me to be on my guard as the Holy Spirit leads.

I need to be always on my guard. God wants to prepare me for what is coming next!

My prayer is that my story brought you joy, laughter, healing, guidance, and comfort. But hopefully, you placed your faith in the Lord Jesus Christ, who has your life in His hands. Trust Him to work out all the details in His timing. Remember that religion cannot heal you, *but Jesus can*! Look to Him.

"Praise be to the God and Father of our Lord Jesus Christ, the Father of compassion and the God of all comfort, who comforts us in all our troubles, so that we can comfort

those in any trouble with the comfort we ourselves have received from God." 2 Corinthians 1:3-4 AMEN

The Lord Has Now Given Me the Peace That Surpasses All Understanding!

"Now may the Lord of peace Himself give you peace at all times and in every way. The Lord be will you all." 2 Thessalonians 3:16

REFERENCES

Bennett, Rita. (1998). *You Can Be Emotionally Free.* Orlando: Bridge-Logos.

Blackaby, H. (1990). *Experiencing God: Knowing and Doing the WIll of God.* Nashville: Life Way Press.

Blackaby, H., & King, C. (2005). *Experiencing God: Youth Edition.* Nashville: Life Way International.

Prince, Derek. (2006). *Blessing or Curse: You Choose.* Grand Rapids: Baker Book House.

Virkler, Mark & Patti. (1989). *Counseled by God.* Shippensburg: Destiny Image Publishing.

Virkler, Mark & Patti. (2001) *Prayers That Heals the Heart.* Newberry: Bridge Logos Publishing.

ADDITIONAL RESOURCES

If you would like to go even deeper, and you haven't yet downloaded the companion Study Guide that goes with my story, would you take a moment and get it? It's my gift to you for reading and I know it will deeply impact your faith and relationship with God. Get the Study Guide at: *bwicministries.com/studyguide*.

As an author, it's often difficult to reach a wider audience on your own. Therefore, I have chosen to partner with BWIC Ministries. I very much believe in their work, mission, and passion for our Lord. I highly recommend checking out their resources, outreach opportunities, and their resources as well. Go to: *bwicministries.com*.

One resource I share quite often is the *Experiencing God* study done by Henry, Richard, and Mike Blackaby and Claude V. King, which has deeply impacted my life and walk with God. I recommend also doing this study, which you can get a copy of at: *amazon.com/dp/1087741688*.

May you be blessed continually and may God get the glory through your life.

THANK YOU

Thank you so much for reading my story. If you were touched, encouraged, or had your own healing experience through reading, would you share your honest review on the book page? It will help my story to reach more people and touch their lives.

To leave a review, go to: *amazon.com/dp/B0DFRPST33*.

If you like, I would also love to hear about your experience personally. Please feel free to send me an e-mail expressing your thoughts at: *Julie51086@gmail.com*.

I will consider using it when updating the book in the future to impact the life of many more people for Christ.

www.ingramcontent.com/pod-product-compliance
Lightning Source LLC
Chambersburg PA
CBHW060326130626
46553CB00003B/939